THRIVING!

How to Create a Healthier, Happier, and More Prosperous Life

Rand Selig

Praise for *Thriving!*

"Rand Selig's wonderful book illuminates the power we have to make positive choices that affect ourselves, others, and the world. Filled with wisdom and practical tools, Thriving! is a valuable compass for navigating life's journey through numerous challenges, occasional setbacks, endings and new beginnings. A must read!"

—Chip Conley, New York Times bestselling author of Peak, Emotional Equations, and Wisdom@Work and founder of MEA

"Thriving! is an enriching journey into the heart of personal growth, empowering readers to carve out their own paths toward a more meaningful and fulfilling existence. This multifaceted exploration ranges from building personal character, cultivating a fruitful relationship with oneself and others, and explores how love, empathy, fear, and the very process of aging shape our existence. Thriving! is packed with insightful guidance and practical tips."

—Scott Allan, best selling author of Do the Hard Things First

"Thriving! is essentially a playbook for being the architect of your own future, living vigorously and identifying who you really are. For those seeking more agency in their lives, Thriving! will feel empowering, honest and pragmatic. Through a variety of techniques, Rand Selig guides you gently into self-discovery and towards the best version of yourself. It's a journey toward both the peace and the awe of living fully in this world."

—Maria Ansari, M.D., CEO of the Permanente Medical Group, Kaiser Permanente

"If you're going to read a book about how to live, inspect the life of the author. Such inspection of Rand Selig will reveal a well-rounded, self-aware, wholly intentional, broadly successful - and thriving - person. In Thriving! he has assembled expertly curated and highly applicable wisdom about how to live. His life skills are beautifully complemented by his financial acumen, articulateness, and managerial and leadership expertise. Don't hesitate to jump in."

—**Dave Evans, Co-founder, Stanford Life Design Lab and Co-author of New York Times bestsellers Designing Your Life, and Designing Your New Work Life**

"Thriving is a choice - a choice that you get to make every day. This book provides a powerful set of insights and tools for claiming agency and meaning in your life. Each page offers valuable wisdom that can be applied right away."

—**Tina L. Seelig, PhD, Executive Director, Knight-Hennessy Scholars and New York Times bestselling author of What I Wish I Knew When I Was 20**

"Rand Selig's Thriving! is an insightful and powerful narrative about the choices, challenges and opportunities we all face in our lives. Through his engaging personal stories and wisdom, Rand creates a pathway for us to examine our own life's journey and make wise choices that will not only enhance our happiness and fulfillment, but also improve our relationships with others and be of service to society. A must read for anyone interested in their personal growth and living a full life!"

—**Andrés R. Edwards, author of Renewal: How Nature Awakens Our Creativity, Compassion, and Joy**

ISBN: 979-8-88759-868-0 (Paperback)

ISBN: 979-8-88759-947-2 (Hardcover)

ISBN: 979-8-88759-869-7 (Ebook)

Library of Congress Control Number: 202 3911 325

Printed in the United States of America.

First printing edition 2023.

www.randselig.com

To everyone who loved me into being and helped me to thrive

I want to thank all of my teachers—formal and informal—in school, at university, in the workplace, and throughout my life. My first teachers were my mother and father.

Thriving!

Are you thriving personally?

Are you thriving in your relationships with friends, family, and partners?

Are you thriving at work, in your career, and financially?

Are you thriving by being actively engaged in the world?

Are you thriving as you move forward in life, regardless of your stage in life?

If you answered no to any of these questions, this book is for you.

Thriving! shows you how you can be the author of your own story.

"To laugh often and much; to win the respect of intelligent people and the affection of children; to earn the appreciation of honest critics and endure the betrayal of false friends; to appreciate beauty; to find the best in others; to leave the world a bit better, whether by a healthy child, a garden, or a redeemed social condition; to know even one life has breathed easier because you have lived. This is to have succeeded."

Ralph Waldo Emerson

Thriving!

- Personally -

- With Others -

- In the World -

- By Moving Ever Forward -

How to Create
a Healthier, Happier,
and More Prosperous Life

Table of Contents

GOOD CARDS? BAD CARDS? PLAYING THEM WELL?

Was I in the right room for my reunion? As I looked around, I saw people whose bodies and faces had borne stress, trauma, and unhappiness. I continued to scan, and I saw other people smiling and radiating vitality. Looking closer, I recognized several classmates. Yes, I was in the right room. And so we begin.

As I realized at my 40th business school reunion, life is a function of two things: First, we're metaphorically dealt cards throughout life, some of which are good, some not so good. Then, second, there's the question of how we play the cards we're dealt. Of course, we'd all love to get good cards and play them well. Maybe we get good cards because we're in the right place at the right time. Perhaps things unfold well without our having to think or work very hard. Then, too, getting a bad hand might not be entirely out of our control. It's well worth considering how many of the bad cards come to us, maybe repeatedly, because of things we could have avoided, possibly by learning from earlier experiences.

Playing our cards well depends on many things, including our personal qualities and character—traits like grit, perseverance, and a moral compass—and whether we have a partner or other support we can count on. But it is also quite possible to fail to play good cards well. Maybe we fold at the wrong moment, or perhaps we aren't prepared. Or maybe we don't have the right mix of character, talent, and skills to get us through. And, sadly, some people are dealt bad cards and then play them poorly.

While we all encounter adversities in the span of a lifetime, this book is about making choices and creating habits that help us get more good cards than bad, and playing the cards we're dealt in life with as much choice, courage, and positive outcome as possible. We'll also examine the many things that can empower and enable us to make choices, as well as the things that hold us back and block us from making the best choices. With a strong foundation rooted in good habits, character, and a positive outlook, I believe each of us can enable or unblock our power to make choices in order to thrive.

Some people thrive, while others go through life without fully living—or, worse, they struggle at every turn. When we are thriving, we are living vigorously. We are flourishing. We are prospering. Are you thriving? If you are, I'm sure you'd like to stay that way. Do you know what choices you've made to bring you to this point of thriving? This book might help you sort through what has been involved so that you have a better chance of remaining in or returning to that fabulous state.

And by the way, thriving is akin to climate, not the weather. On any given day (the weather), things might not be going so well, and we may be struggling in some way. But on average, over a more extended period (climate), we can live vigorously, flourish, and prosper. That is thriving. Thriving happens when the frequency of positive is vastly greater than the frequency of negative.

What if you are not thriving? Do you know why not? Do you know what choices you can make to move toward a happier, healthier, and more prosperous life? There are specific things we can do to make ourselves whole and alive, just as there are many things we can do to make ourselves miserable. It can be argued that the amount of work to achieve either—wholeness or despair—is the same. This book's goal is to help you sort through the complexities of your life and illuminate a path forward into a state of thriving.

This book is organized into four sections. Section I is about the ingredients needed to thrive personally. It examines our many choices to be happy, healthy, and prosperous. Because these are foundational elements of a life well lived, the first 8 of the 15 chapters of this book are about thriving personally.

Section II builds on Section I and is about creating thriving relationships with others—our partners and families, as well as in our work as followers, managers, or leaders.

Section III is directed toward thriving in the world around us by using our time, talents, and financial resources to help others and our precious natural world.

The last portion of this book, Section IV, addresses the vital processes and choices involved with thriving as we continue to move through life. This includes evolving to become a better person and gaining wisdom.

The last chapter wraps up with a proviso: we can tap into our power to thrive, but only if we take hold of the reins by doing the hard work of knowing ourselves, taking responsibility, summoning our courage, and making the often hard choices along the way.

This book is expressly designed to be a workbook. In each chapter, there are questions raised for the reader. These are not rhetorical. They are invitations meant to engage you to make these life topics real and personal so that they lead to action. I encourage you to spend time with them. Don't rush. Maybe pause between chapters or sections. I recommend having a notepad or journal (paper or electronic) with you as you work through this book.

As you will see, I love quotes. These are meant to enhance the material in each chapter. The quotes I've chosen range from very succinct and on point to more lighthearted and humorous. They include thoughts from philosophers, religious figures, generals, business and political leaders, writers, and even comedians and entertainers. Also included in some chapters are prayers and poems.

While my perspective reflects the life I have lived so far, which in many ways is one of success, health, and happiness, my view also reflects the struggles I have overcome. Life for me has not been all "peaches and cream." I grew up in a middle-class family, with both my parents working. Key among the challenges I overcame was a difficult relationship with my father, whom I didn't get to know until I was eight years old and who is a strong-willed, forceful, and relatively emotionally distant person. I am grateful to have a loving mother who was always in my father's shadow. This was often painful to watch and diminished the support I sometimes needed from her. All of this illustrates that our family dynamic and history don't determine our future. Each of us does.

The second key challenge I have had to handle is physical. For all my adult life, I have had a limiting and at times painful chronic autoimmune eye condition. This started in my early 20s and was exacerbated by a stressful career. Adding to these two struggles, I have a strong personality, which has included being judgmental and demanding, needing control, and exhibiting limited emotional empathy for others. While my personality has lent itself to certain kinds of accomplishments, at the same time, it created problems within my family and with other important relationships.

The critical point to note, however, is that with a commitment and belief in myself, and a lot of work over many years, I have been able to overcome these challenges. Without these adversities, I certainly would not have become the person I am today. Because of the difficulties I encountered growing up and then as I aged and took on more responsibilities, I am sure that I became a better father and was able to consciously design a life for myself and my family that aligned with my values. I took control of my career and obtained financial success by running my own firm based on clear principles. And, very importantly, I developed more compassion, humility, and gratitude over time. Overcoming my challenges has led to a more well-rounded, balanced, integrated, authentic, and happy life. I hope my story will empower you.

It is understandable that a reader might be naturally drawn to some chapters and some points and less so, or not at all, to other chapters or points. That's perfectly fine. Additionally, some topics may resonate more at certain junctures in a person's life. Again, perfectly understandable. Maybe over a long period—decades, even—possibly because you are in another stage of life facing different challenges, you might return to this book and engage with other chapters and topics. And you may feel that this book would be good for a family member or friend, maybe someone younger or older than you.

If you're like me, you might be tempted to skip the endnotes and the list of recommended books. Many of these books significantly helped me become the person I am today. I urge you to spend time with these sections of this book as well. I am confident they will enhance your access to and appreciation of the issues I've written about.

This is a book of ideas and possibilities, which includes a set of philosophies, frameworks, models, and best practices. These might provide you with scaffolding that could help support the design, enhancement, or improvement of your life. *Thriving!* is fundamentally about making the choices that allow you to live a healthy, productive, and happy life.

Shakespeare's Hamlet famously said, "To be, or not to be, that is the question." This book is about **how** to be. Throughout, it is relentlessly positive. The book's chapters identify significant issues about a life I have endeavored to live well and fully. Hopefully, as the reader, you will benefit from this book and avoid some of the traps I have fallen into. Or maybe you will pick up some ideas that will help you accelerate and expand your process of becoming a wonderful person and even reach your potential. The world needs it! May your journey be a good one. As *Star Trek*'s Mr. Spock says when he raises one hand in the Vulcan salute, "Live long and prosper."

Rand Selig   *Mill Valley, California*   *August 2023*

SECTION I

THRIVING PERSONALLY

*"**Keep your thoughts positive, because your thoughts become your words.**
Keep your words positive, because your words become your behavior.
Keep your behavior positive, because your behavior becomes your habits.
Keep your habits positive, because your habits become your values.
Keep your values positive, because your values become your destiny."*

Mahatma Gandhi, in his retirement speech to the first freely elected parliament of India

Thriving Personally

1 - Building Character

2 - Relationship with Ourselves

3 - Managing Ourselves

4 - Money

5 - Emotions

Happiness, Love, Trust, Empathy and Compassion, Vulnerability, Forgiveness, Emotional Upset or Anger, Fear, Feelings about Dying, Inner Peace

6 - Spirituality and Religion

7 - Gratitude

8 - Purpose and Meaning

1

BUILDING CHARACTER

"Life is like a grindstone. It will grind you down into grains of sand, or it will polish you like a beautiful gem. It all depends on what you are made of."

Lavey Derby

An essential aspect of thriving personally is building character. This means, first, that we have to know who we are by becoming self-aware. This work involves assessing our personality, along with recognizing our strengths and weaknesses. Building character also requires us to clarify our values and what we stand for. These are not simple or obvious things to be clear about.

All of this takes significant work and honest self-assessment. There are, however, enormous benefits to becoming self-aware and clarifying our values. We can become stronger and more able to overcome obstacles, difficult times, and difficult people. This clarity can also lead to more life satisfaction, authenticity, achievement, and happiness. Conversely, it can be argued that a life without thorough examination does not lead to a meaningful existence.

A person of character also continues to grow and learn throughout their life. This, too, takes commitment and requires us to take some risks. People who have the courage to be fully themselves are often the happiest and most content.

Personality

"Pressure is a privilege." Billie Jean King

Let's start by taking a look at the elements of personality. Consider them building blocks. Research points to the possibility that personality traits can change through persistent intervention and major life events. The five major personality factors often referred to with the acronym **OCEAN** are considered to be:

O—Openness to experience—how curious, adventurous, intelligent, creative, and receptive we are to new ideas, emotions, and experiences, as opposed to being uninquisitive, dumb, and uncreative.

C—Conscientiousness—how organized, efficient, responsible, careful, practical, and committed we are to finishing projects or reaching our goals, versus the opposites of being disorganized, irresponsible, sloppy, and impractical.

E—Extroversion/introversion—how outgoing, social, talkative, or full of energy we are in social settings, as opposed to being quiet, reserved, and more inclined to listen than speak. Introverts' energy recharges with solitude, whereas extroverts' energy recharges with social interactions.

A—Agreeableness/disagreeableness—how warm, friendly, cooperative, helpful, generous, and tactful we are, versus the opposites of being cold, adversarial, and stingy.

N—Neuroticism/emotional stability—how calm, stable, content, and unflappable we are, versus being anxious, discontented, angry, jealous, lonely, or insecure.

How does your personality stack up in terms of these factors? You can take a free test by going to https://www.truity.com/test/big-five-personality-test. It takes 5 to 10 minutes.

As you review where you are with each of these personality factors, what are you most pleased about? What do you want to work on?

Each of these OCEAN personality factors expresses a spectrum, with one end of the spectrum generally viewed in our society as good and the other end as bad. The extroversion/introversion spectrum is different, however, as neither trait is necessarily good or bad. There are advantages and disadvantages to both. Besides significant differences in how extroverts and introverts act, a major difference is in what situations they thrive and get energy. Because we live in an extroverted society with only an estimated 25 percent to 40 percent of people testing as introverts, it's essential to know whether we are extroverted, introverted, or some hybrid of the two.

According to a well-known personality assessment tool known as the Myers-Briggs Type Indicator, I am an INTJ—a problem solver and an introvert driven by extroverted thinking. As a dominant introverted intuitive, I do my best work preparing and thinking things through alone. While I enjoy being with small groups, I prefer one-on-one interactions. I don't like being unprepared and always create and share a written meeting agenda. After lots of social time, I need to withdraw and recharge my battery. This means that I am introverted but also social, not shy.

Introverts have the advantage of seeing many sides of an issue; not relying on pure rationality; being nonlinear at times; having the ability to be flexible; being creative (thinking out of the box); going deep if needed; and seeking renewal. By honoring your introverted, intuitive self, you can wait for resolutions to emerge from within and get to know your own individual and personal truth. This allows you to feel less driven and more playful, creative, and authentic.

If you are struggling with being an introvert in an extroverted world, I highly recommend the book *Quiet: The Power of Introverts in a World That Can't Stop Talking*, by Susan Cain. Here are a few suggestions: First, determine whether you are introverted, extroverted, or both. Sort out what environment you function best in. Second, if you are introverted, it will help you to work far less in groups—such as in schools and offices. Settings that are more solitary will allow for more of the privacy and autonomy you need. Having solitude leads to creativity. And third, unplug from the daily hustle and bustle of a noisy life and go into nature. By being alone and getting into your head, you'll increase your chances of having insights and revelations.

It is important to note that being alone periodically and having solitude is something extroverts, too, are highly likely to benefit from.

Are you primarily extroverted or introverted? There are several tests you can take. One of these is short and free at www.introvertdear.com.

With this knowledge of our personality traits, let's now investigate character. According to various studies, the following seven character strengths are believed to be most likely to predict life satisfaction and achievement:

Zest—Those who have zest exude enthusiasm, excitement, and energy when approaching things in life. This quality minimizes focusing on negative views. Instead, zest involves performing tasks wholeheartedly while also being adventurous, vivacious, and energetic.

Grit—Having grit and resilience is essential in the complicated, messy world we live in. Grit and resilience require us to be mentally tough. This is further discussed below. Remember that persistence can lead to success, as we often need only one yes. We might have to struggle through many rejections or noes before we get the one yes. We have probably all heard "If at first you don't succeed, try, try again." I believe the only real way to fail is not to try. For me, much of my career success has been based on persistence. With grit in mind, I especially like the quote by Winston Churchill "If you're going through hell, keep going."

Optimism—Studies show that being optimistic and cheerful adds eight to nine years to our lives. Optimism gives us power and is a critical ingredient in our belief that we can design our own lives. Fear and pessimism diminish power. I am naturally optimistic and often tell family and friends, "Life is good." Be aware that hope is not the same as optimism, although they are often used interchangeably. We can always be hopeful, but we may not think the future looks promising; hence we might not be optimistic. **Are you a glass-half-full person? Or half-empty?**

Gratitude—Gratitude is being thankful and showing appreciation. Feeling grateful for something or someone leads to feelings of kindness and warmth, and spurs various forms of generosity. For more on this, see chapter 7.

Curiosity—Curious people have the desire to learn and investigate. They enjoy novel and unexpected things. This trait makes our minds stronger, and we generally become more observant.

Social intelligence—This is the ability to communicate and form relationships with an appropriate balance between empathy and assertiveness. It comes from knowing ourselves and being self-aware.

Self-control—This is the ability to exercise restraint over ourselves—including our emotions, desires, actions, and impulses—especially in difficult situations.

And an eighth strength: humor—To the seven character-building qualities above, I will add the importance of a sense of humor, both about situations and about ourselves.

Which of these do you almost always have? Which ones rarely? To which of them do you attribute your achievement and life satisfaction? What do you want to work on?

In order to thrive, being mentally, psychologically strong and resilient—that is, having grit—is a critical character quality to hone. How does a person become strong and resilient? There are two primary ways: One is by overcoming a difficult situation, even near death, by being firm, steadfast, and sometimes forceful. I call this strong like an oak. While this approach certainly can be beneficial at times, it's essential to be aware that this kind of strength can lead to rigidity, stubbornness, and being demanding of others, along with other undesirable personal qualities. My father's strength came from this quality of steadfastness, and he passed on to me this approach to being strong.

The other way a person can become mentally and psychologically strong is by what I call "cradling," which is to be deeply loved and cared for by others, or maybe only one other person. I call this willow-branch strength. In this case, our strength and resilience come from having confidence that there is always someone around and available who will care about us and help us if we get into difficulty. For me, this was my mother. So, it's important and valuable to be mentally strong but flexible. I am very thankful to be strong in both ways, and as I have aged and matured, I see that much of my strength and resilience come more from the willow.

Do you have grit? Are you strong like an oak or like a willow branch? Give examples.

Here are some suggestions from motivational speaker and author Jon Gordon on being mentally tough:[1]

Adversity

When you encounter difficulties, embrace them, understanding that they're not roadblocks but rather opportunities for growth and improvement. When faced with setbacks, think of them as defining moments that will lead to future successes. When experiencing failure, learn from it, and then remember a time when you have succeeded. And remember that we learn more from criticism than from praise.

Negative People

When you face the naysayers, remember the people who believed in you and spoke positive words to you. When you face critics, remember to tune them out and focus only on being the best you can be. Remember that everyone will have to overcome negativity to define themselves and create their own success.

Focus

When you feel overwhelmed, focus on what you can control, and let go of what you can't. When feeling distracted, use your breath to focus on the present moment, observe your surroundings, and clear your mind. Instead of dwelling on the past or worrying about the future, focus your energy on the present moment.

Be Positive

When self-doubt arises, replace it with positive self-talk and thoughts. Instead of complaining, identify a solution. When under pressure, remember to smile, have fun, and try to enjoy the situation.

Do Your Best and Finish Strong

Always doing one's best is a mark of a person with strong character. And even when you are tired and drained, remember to never, never, never give up. I was raised with this ethic stamped into me. When I was a young boy in New Mexico, my mom would give my sister and me weekly chores to do. If we didn't complete them correctly, we would have to do them again until they were done well. From the time I was 10, my father had me shine his army shoes and boots (10 cents per pair of shoes; 25 cents for boots). They had to pass inspection. Later in life, when my wife and I lived in Tokyo, we appreciated the taxi drivers who drove their very clean taxis with pride, wearing white gloves and keeping a feather duster on the back shelf. From these experiences and many others, I realized that no matter what we decide to do in our work and in any other aspect of our lives, it's essential always to do our best and finish strong.

In which ways are you mentally tough?

Another aspect of personality and character is something called presence. Generally, if we are thriving, we will have more presence. Presence is a combination of several key things, including being:

Confident   **Passionate**   **Enthusiastic**

Authentic   **Captivating**   **Comfortable**

Hopefully these are understandable terms. A few comments: Being authentic is first about being self-aware and then having the courage to be yourself. Regarding enthusiasm, I love Coach Jim Harbaugh's encouragement "Attack this day with enthusiasm unknown to mankind." And my son, who has a lot of presence, likes to say, "Because every day is an adventure!"

Do you have presence? In which of its key elements are you strongest? Less strong?

The good news is that we don't need to be the most intelligent or talented person to achieve success and thrive in life. Often it's the seemingly simple things, things that don't cost money but do require intentionality and effort, that can make a significant difference. Here, based on an article by Jon Gordon, are 10 things anyone can do.[2]

1. **Be on time**—Respect others by being punctual, as showing up on time shows that you value the other person's time. This can help earn you respect in return.

2. **Show up and do the work**—Do the work consistently and persistently, regardless of whether you receive praise or criticism, and even if you are ignored or unnoticed.

3. **Give your best in all that you do**—Put forth your best effort in everything you do and focus on your contribution, regardless

of others' actions. By doing so, you'll inspire others to do the same.

4. **Do more than what's required**—Exceed expectations by going above and beyond what is required and striving to achieve more. Average effort generates average results and rewards, but putting in a little extra each day can lead to big results over time.

5. **Seek solutions**—Find solutions instead of dwelling on problems. This approach can reveal a wide range of possibilities and help overcome challenges.

6. **Be coachable**—Remain open to learning and improvement by staying humble and eager to learn from others and your own mistakes. Approach life as a continuous learning journey.

7. **Be positively contagious**—Spread positivity by actively seeking ways to support and inspire those around you. Your attitude has the power to influence others.

8. **Have an attitude of gratitude**—Choose to have a grateful attitude and focus on the good things, rather than letting negative emotions such as anger, fear, doubt, and insecurity steal your joy and prevent you from living the life you're meant to live.

9. **Have passion**—Passion drives success and fulfillment. It fuels your purpose and helps you thrive, not just survive.

10. **Believe in yourself**—Feed the positive and stop listening to the self-sabotaging voices in your mind. Remind yourself that you matter, you are capable of great things, and you have a purpose.

Which of these do you routinely do? What would you like to do more of?

Many things in life happen to us that are out of our control. Severe accidents, chronic illness, and adverse childhood experiences (ACE)[3] are examples. An ACE score is a tally of different types of abuse, neglect, and other hallmarks of a rough childhood. You can take the ACE quiz by going to https://www.npr.org/sections/health-shots/2015/03/02/387007941/take-the-ace-quiz-and-learn-what-it-does-and-doesnt-mean. Some adults who had ACEs become "dandelions" and can overcome many obstacles in their lives, while other people become "orchids" and wilt under stress or challenge. Growing up, I had a series of adverse childhood experiences, scoring 3 out of 10 on the ACE test, but I am fortunate to be a dandelion. While we might not control the things that are out of our control, to some degree we might be able to determine how we deal with these events and conditions. We make choices all along the way when we face adversity. Will we wilt and avoid? Or will we engage and attempt to overcome? Again, it may be possible to change how we deal with these kinds of things with effort over time.

How do you score on the ACE quiz? Because of childhood experiences, what personality or character qualities do you have that are unhelpful to you? How are you addressing these?

In addition to things out of our control, there may be some less attractive, unhelpful character components we might have developed as adults. One example is how we think about the things that we get. I have heard that there are three very different kinds of people: Some people think they're getting what they deserve and feel entitled or narcissistic. Others think they are getting what they can get away with, and as a result, they may not have much integrity or be very trustworthy. And still others think they get what they negotiate. These people may use power in poor and selfish ways.

Which are you? How is that working out for you?

Virtues, Values, and Principles

"Live in such a way that if someone spoke badly about you, no one would believe it." Zig Ziglar

Now let's turn to virtues and values. They are deeply linked to our character. Virtues are qualities that are universally considered to be good and desirable. Values are principles or standards of behavior that can help us decide what's important in life. They reflect what we stand for and what we won't stand for. They open us to many choices, allowing us to choose to engage in life with a view that this is a time to work, a time to play, a time to live, and a time to love and be at peace. Our values and virtues can enable us to thrive in our place on this great planet hurtling through space and time.

Regarding virtues, a description of seven venerable virtues follows.

Humility—humbleness and freedom from pride or arrogance

Generosity—intentionally giving our time, treasure, and talent

Restraint—controlling our most passionate impulses

Kindness—tolerating the mistakes of our fellow humans

Moderation—satisfying ourselves with the necessities

Charity—helping those who are unable to help themselves

Diligence—making ourselves useful in the modern world

Consider each of the virtues above. Which virtues are you living? Think of examples.

When considering our values, Rushworth Kidder wrote that the following are the shared values needed in a troubled world. These constitute a global code of ethics. Note: Go slowly through each of these. Pause and reflect before going on to the next one.

Love

Truthfulness

Fairness

Freedom

Unity

Tolerance

Responsibility*

Respect for life[4]

Which of the above values are most important to you? What values are you living?

*** A special note on responsibility:** The one quality that all successful people have is the ability to take on responsibility. In general, when we take responsibility, we have the ability to choose how to respond to what's going on rather than feel the compulsion to react. To be successful and thrive, we need to be responsible people. This includes taking responsibility for our own actions and not blaming others.

Another way to recognize what we value is to note what gives us goosebumps. For me, this includes being in nature, seeing animals, and seeing incredible vistas. It includes feeling and observing strong emotions like love, sorrow, and happiness. I get goosebumps when I see parents and children happily together. People giving the best of themselves give me goosebumps when they are helping others, caring, going out of their way, and being selfless. I get chills when I observe the fulfillment of responsibility—making and keeping commitments: "You can count on me. If you need me, I'll be there." Excellence in work well done, in leadership, management, art, performing arts, scholarship, or athletics, is another. And I certainly get goosebumps with the triumph of good over evil, with life over death, and when I see the indomitable human spirit.

What gives you goosebumps? What do you value?

Now let's talk about principles. It's important to know what principles are guiding our lives. Knowing them can lead to focus and impact. Helpful principles can lead us to life satisfaction. Our principles can help us decide how to act, how to spend our time, and with whom. Consider as examples developing a life based on being kind and caring, creating loving relationships, being a supportive and loyal friend, and being compassionate, passionate, and authentic.

Another thing to consider in creating a principle-based ideal life is that our work is meaningful and serves a good purpose. This leads to choices about how, where, and why we contribute our time, talent, experience, skills, and "life force." When I started my own firm many years ago, I developed a set of clear principles we would apply to our work. These involved creating quality relationships and providing more than functional and technical competence. They have served us well and allowed us to avoid many potential problems.

Our principles can also lead us to choose how we spend our

nonworking time. We can choose to volunteer on projects to repair the world in any number of ways, including building community, serving others, and being charitable and philanthropic. To have an ideal life, also consider having a central principle of experiencing and appreciating a closeness to nature and caring for Mother Earth. We can do this by rolling up our sleeves and planting trees, cleaning up beaches, and volunteering on other environmental service projects. Importantly, this principle leads to considering the environmental impacts of what we consume and the things we purchase. And in turn, this means being financially responsible by spending less than we earn, buying only what we can afford, and managing our financial affairs well. This is discussed in greater detail in chapters 4, 11, and 12.

To regularly and routinely do these things—to live our values and principles—we need to be mentally, physically, spiritually, and emotionally healthy. It requires us to be very conscious of and disciplined about spending our time on things that are important, recognizing that time is a scarce resource. For me, I am trying to live every day with little as well as with bigger things so that I can be the change I wish to see in the world. I am attempting to live my life based on principles of excellence, purpose, encouragement, and love.

What principles are guiding your life? I recommend devoting the time to consider this carefully and writing them down.

Being a Lifelong Learner

"Real education consists in drawing the best out of yourself."
Mahatma Gandhi

Being a lifelong learner requires us to continually learn about ourselves, about others, and about the world and how it works. This includes being curious, listening, asking questions, watching, and reading. To achieve real learning, though, involves experiencing things personally and teaching others. An eye-opening study by William Glasser about how we learn revealed that we learn:

10 percent of what we read

20 percent of what we hear

30 percent of what we see

50 percent of what we both hear and see

70 percent of what we experience personally

95 percent of what we *teach* to someone else

How do you learn? What can you do to learn more?

Remember that it's not how far we've traveled in life, it's what we've brought back that counts. Being a lifelong learner means understanding our experiences and learning from our successes, but especially from our failures and mistakes. It also requires us to take a look at our shortcomings. We should not ignore or feel embarrassed by our difficulties. Instead, we should attempt to grow something beautiful from them.

As I consider my own life, I realize I have had a number of short-comings, which have included being too demanding; being too opinionated and judgmental; not forgiving enough or soon enough; not being patient enough; not achieving enough of a balance between patience and my drive to get things done correctly and in a timely fashion; being vulnerable to people who were hostile to my vision; and altogether not being naturally empathetic.

I hope and believe that my awareness of these things and my hard work to overcome them has made them less of an impediment to my relationships and the work I do.

Do any of these sound familiar in your life? What are your shortcomings? What are your plans to correct them?

When we make a mistake, we become stronger by reviewing how it happened and what we could have done differently. When you're facing up to a mistake or suffering a setback, it might be valuable to remember this acronym:

LOSS is a learning opportunity:

L—Learning

O—Opportunity

S—Stay

S—Strong

What mistakes have you made? Be honest. Write them down. What did you learn from them?

Being a lifelong learner often requires a willingness to change and to take risks, recognizing that trying something new may be uncomfortable. But by doing so, we can become stronger and evolve into being a better person. As I have gone through life and had countless experiences, mostly good but with periodic setbacks and mistakes, I have grown and evolved. This was possible only by being committed to being a lifelong learner willing to learn from my mistakes and weaknesses and taking appropriate risks to change. This is discussed in more detail in chapter 13.

In what ways are you a lifelong learner? How are you changing and evolving?

2

RELATIONSHIP WITH OURSELVES

"The thing that is really hard, and really amazing, is giving up on being perfect and beginning the work of becoming yourself."

Anna Quindlen

A critical aspect of thriving personally is to have a deep and caring relationship with ourselves. Of all the relationships we'll have in our lives, the most important relationship we'll ever have is the one with ourselves. Before we can have significant, meaningful, and lasting relationships with others, a strong and loving relationship with ourselves is necessary.

Like assessing your personality and values in chapter 1, becoming self-aware about your relationship with yourself is invaluable homework to do. In our relationship with ourselves, we can look at each aspect of self: the physical self, the emotional self, the social self, the intellectual self, and the spiritual self. It might take courage for honest self-examination.

As we grow and develop, and as we make important choices about ourselves, including the choice to renew ourselves routinely, there are many things we can do to age well. These are discussed below.

Growing and Developing

"Don't accept your dog's admiration as conclusive evidence that you are wonderful." Ann Landers

Developing a healthy relationship with ourselves is thought to be positive development. According to developmental psychologist Erik Erikson,[5] the following five aspects are involved in the growth and crises for a healthy personality from birth to adolescence:

Basic trust—reasonable trustfulness of others, without being mistrustful; being a trustworthy person

Autonomy—sense of rightful dignity and lawful independence, without shame and doubt

Initiative—self-activated; forget failures quickly and approach what seems desirable with undiminished and better-aimed effort, without guilt

Industry—learn and accomplish, solitary and communal, work and play, without feeling inferior

Identity—knowing who one is and being comfortable with not having to rebel or being in the way of what others want, without being lost

These first five stages are followed in adulthood by

Intimacy (versus isolation), which Erikson says can lead to being able to give and receive love

Generativity (versus stagnation), which leads to caring for people besides ourselves and family, as well as caring for and contributing to the life of the next generation

Ego integration (versus despair), which involves organizing drives, attitudes, and aims into a balanced whole; this leads to wisdom

How do you assess yourself on these eight factors? Which aspects do you still find challenging?

Another, but similar, set of indicators of well-being can help us assess our relationship with ourselves. Having these helps us to have strong character and to thrive. We are much more likely to struggle if we don't have these characteristics. These key indicators include:

Self-regard—liking most aspects of our personality

Control of our life—taking responsibility for ourselves, setting meaningful goals, connecting to our values

Autonomy—having confidence in our opinions even if they're contrary to the general consensus

Supportive social relationships (see chapter 9, Relationships with Others)

Personal growth—having new experiences that challenge how we think and feel about ourselves

Sense of purpose (see chapter 8, Purpose and Meaning)

Take a look at each of these indicators. Which are solid for you? Which need attention?

Having a healthy sense of self is essential. Central to this is self-esteem and self-awareness, but not the kind of self-absorption that is antithetical to relationships and community. We do not have to achieve perfect self-confidence and centeredness. Knowing what we want, what our strengths and limitations are, and how we plan to grow is helpful. We need to be secure enough to avoid having to defend, protect, or prove ourselves constantly.

Keeping a journal is very valuable to help navigate through all of the above questions and the assessment process overall, especially when there is a lot of complexity involved or when we are troubled or confused. It also helps to check in periodically with ourselves. This is not easy to do. Have courage. This can also be a great conversation to have with a partner or a close friend. Ask these questions:

On a scale of 1 to 10, how are you today? How does this compare to your average set point? Why are you today above or below your average set point?

Making Choices

"Experience is not what happens to you; it is what you do with what happens to you." Aldous Huxley

As we develop our relationship with ourselves, we constantly make choices about our lives. We have an enormous amount of choice regarding how we want to live life and how we want to feel about ourselves and others. A number of these areas of choice are discussed below.

A central component of our relationship with ourselves is our self-compassion. Here are educator and researcher Barbara Larrivee's

Ten Commandments of Self-Compassion.[6] These represent choices too. I have grouped them as positive and negative. Each begins with **Thou shalt . . .**

1. accept yourself completely.
2. schedule time for yourself.
3. give yourself permission to do nothing sometimes.
4. be your own best friend.
5. not say yes when you want to say no.
6. not need to have others' approval.
7. not try to prove yourself to anyone.
8. not aim to be perfect.
9. not be afraid to be wrong.
10. not feel guilty.

Are you self-compassionate? In which ways? What can you do more to be self-compassionate?

According to Bob Hoffman, founder of the Hoffman Process, depending on our early life and later experiences, we may have something called negative love,[7] which is the experience of feeling unlovable. It is an intergenerational pain passed down from one generation to the next. We all have negative moods, attitudes, and behaviors that emanate from a very deep emotional level, but negative love goes well beyond that to reflect our feeling of being unlovable. In every situation when we as children experience a parent's love being cut off—through divorce, abandonment, death, imprisonment, or their love becoming conditional—the parental bond is broken for us. Dealing effectively with negative love might require the help of a trained therapist. We have a choice as to whether and when we work on this.

Is there negative love in your life? With whom? Remember a specific instance. Regardless, do you love yourself? Are you kind to yourself? In which ways?

Because of habits of the mind, we are often our own worst enemies, and we shoot ourselves in the foot. We undermine ourselves with saboteurs, our internal enemies. These are automatic and habitual mind patterns, each with its own voice, beliefs, and assumptions that work against our best interests. Saboteurs are a universal phenomenon. The question is not whether we have them but which ones we have and how strong they are. This is brilliantly described in Shirzad Chamine's *Positive Intelligence: Why Only 20% of Teams and Individuals Achieve Their True Potential and How You Can Achieve Yours.*[8]

The judge is the master saboteur; everyone suffers from it. It leads to a constant focus on finding flaws with ourselves, others, and our situation. It creates a lot of negative emotions such as anxiety, stress, anger, disappointment, shame, and guilt. Its self-justifying lie is that without it, we or others would become lazy and unambitious, and would not achieve much. Its voice is, therefore, often mistaken as a source of guidance and a tough-love voice, when in reality it is a destructive saboteur. The good news is that there are ways to weaken the judge and its nine accomplices.

The sage represents the deeper and wiser part of us. By accessing our inner wisdom, we are able to stay calm and level-headed during difficult situations, instead of getting caught up in the drama and tension of the moment. The sage helps us avoid falling victim to the saboteurs. It sees any challenge as an opportunity or as something that could be actively turned into one. It has access to five great powers of the mind and taps into those powers to meet any challenge.

More good news: these sage powers lie in regions of the brain that are different from the regions that fuel our saboteurs, and there are ways to strengthen and develop the sage's perspective and powers.[9]

What are your saboteurs? How are you shooting yourself in the foot? How are you diminishing your saboteurs and empowering your sage?

Another one of the most critical choices we make is whether or not to feel like a victim. Many things lead to what might be called unfair advantages. The truth is that we all have them, and there is no such thing as a level playing field or an even starting point in life. There are always factors that give someone a head start or a tailwind that propels them forward. Success is always about people leveraging their strengths and their circumstances as they journey through their lives. It's up to us whether we choose to feel like a victim or not. With this in mind, I highly recommend reading Malcolm Gladwell's book *David and Goliath: Underdogs, Misfits, and the Art of Battling Giants.*

Do you have a victim mentality? What are examples of this?

It's vital in our relationship with ourselves to reflect on life's randomness. Some things that happen to us are of our own making, while others are outside our control. If we were to press a global reset button and everyone on the planet were reborn into different circumstances, who'd be lucky then? What obstacles might we have now that we didn't have before? Even with life's randomness, there are underlying choices we can make. Ask yourself these questions:

How many of my difficulties are due to my own behaviors and choices? Give examples.

How much of the success I've had in life was not in my control and was possibly just good luck? What choices did I make? What are a few examples?

Am I choosing to take responsibility for my actions and my life overall? In which ways?

One of the most important choices we can make in life concerns self-renewal. Throughout our journey in life, to thrive we must take care of ourselves physically, mentally, emotionally, and spiritually. The latest research and findings in the fields of psychology, sports, sleep, and physiology illuminate the profound and transformative effects of meditation, mindfulness, unplugging, and giving.

We can consciously renew ourselves, something Stephen Covey refers to in his book *The 7 Habits of Highly Effective People* as "sharpening the saw." Effective self-renewal goes beyond innovation and change, however. It includes ensuring that the results are in line with our purpose.

In which ways are you sharpening your saw? What else can you do to renew?

Critical aspects of self-renewal include relaxing regularly, resting when needed, and sleeping well. I am very fortunate that not only do I sleep well, but as a part of my week, I relax for one day every week and use this time to enjoy food, see friends and family, sleep in, take a hike, and enjoy life. During this time, I do not work or go shopping and do not use a computer or check email. Taking care of ourselves does not require spending much money!

What do you do to renew yourself regularly?

On top of this, consider taking extended time off from work. Some people call this a sabbatical. This involves taking at least 3 months—maybe even 6 to 12 months—away from work and normal day-to-day activities. Don't dismiss this out of hand! It may be more possible financially than you might realize. For example, for our four sabbaticals taken during the pressing family and career period of my 30s and 40s, we rented our house while away and had a sponsoring organization put "skin in the game" by paying for our airfare or by housing and feeding us during our stay.

Such a break can have tremendous benefits, including:
- Recharging mentally and physically
- Reconnecting with our most central relationships—ourselves and our spouse/partner, children, extended family, and friends
- Connecting with our spiritual self
- Trying something new—an adventure, learning, work, or skill
- Being involved with something we care about other than ourselves or family

There are many types of sabbaticals, including working on a service project; getting more education, maybe a certificate or degree; and participating in an exchange program. In the academic world, sabbaticals are common and are usually taken every seven years. The time away can go by amazingly fast, so it's best to have thought out what it is we're trying to achieve with our sabbatical. This is a special time when we can reevaluate specific aspects of our life—the work we're doing, our career, our relationships, what commitments we want to continue to make and new ones to initiate, our values, and taking an honest look at ourselves, among other things. We can return from our time away with a recharged battery and possibly a new motor. I recommend using a journal and taking lots of pictures as well.

What benefits do you imagine you'd experience by taking extended time off and away? What would be required for you to plan this?

Aging Well

"The older the violin, the sweeter the music." Hank Thompson

Naturally, growing and developing include aging. We all do it, but not everyone ages well. As humans, we continue to learn about the true nature of vitality, which is modeled on the natural world. Vitality reflects mutuality and reciprocity. Aging well is central to thriving.

Aging well is thought to consist of these factors: physical health and functional status; mental and cognitive effectiveness; social support, including having friends of all ages; being positive and optimistic; and having a purpose that is greater than self. As a result, we make many choices along the way, even beginning in our 30s and 40s, that lead to aging well. The benefits of aging well are significant and include, among other things, having more energy and stamina, reducing aches and pains, living with more vitality, having a sense of meaning, developing better relationships, and experiencing more happiness and enjoyment in life. With this in mind, I highly recommend reading *Younger Next Year: Live Strong, Fit, Sexy and Smart—Until You're 80 and Beyond*, by Chris Crowley and Henry Lodge, MD.

Are you aging well? In what ways? What choices are you making?

According to psychotherapist Thomas Moore, these are the stages of a healthy life:

1. Educate yourself and develop talents and skills.
2. Look for a job that employs those abilities.
3. Develop a career.
4. Deal with endings and turning points in your career.
5. Achieve success in your own way.
6. Shift, especially with more time in the older years, into an emphasis on service.
7. Create a legacy for future generations.[10]

Moore suggests that aging and maturing often start with feeling immortal. This is followed by a phase when we have the first taste of aging, after which we begin settling into maturity. At some point we shift toward old age. Finally, we enter the phase of letting things take their course.[11] Ram Dass,[12] an American spiritual teacher, said his father was initially a high achiever. As he got older, he started to let go of his need for power and control. And as Ram Dass's father got very old, he let go more and more until he was just a silent, smiling Buddha.

Which stage or phase are you in? What stage do you want to be in?

"Some people grow older in years but don't age well, and their interactions with the world remain immature," as Thomas Moore eloquently writes in *Ageless Soul: The Lifelong Journey toward Meaning and Joy.* They may be active, but their actions lack a deep understanding and connection with the world around them.[13] They stay focused on themselves, lacking empathy and a sense of community. They are unable to open themselves emotionally to others and can't form deep connections. They tend to hold on to anger and other negative emotions rather than processing and releasing them. They may have developed coping mechanisms to avoid dealing with their emotions, and over time, they may have lost the motivation or hope for personal growth and maturity. As Benjamin Franklin said, "Many people die at 25 and aren't buried until they're 75." However, none of these things are inevitable—it is possible to age well.

As discussed in Daniel Levitin's *Successful Aging: A Neuroscientist Explores the Power and Potential of Our Lives,*[14] having curiosity, openness, associations (as in sociability), conscientiousness, and healthy practices are the five lifestyle choices that have the most significant impact on the rest of our lives. (Levitin refers to these with the acronym COACH.) All of these, except for maintaining healthy practices, are described in chapter 1 of *Thriving!*

As we go through life, several possibilities describe aging well. When we age successfully, we stay engaged and active, and our life finds purpose and meaning. That depth of being is a tremendous gift to ourselves. To age well, we must allow ourselves to be impacted by our experiences and be open to learning and growth so that we feel ourselves sprouting and blossoming. And bad times can make good times even more beautiful.

As Thomas Moore writes in *Ageless Soul,* "There can be a joy of aging. We can become a real person, someone with individual judgment, a particular outlook on life, and a set of values to believe in. The soul blooms with a profound sense of self, and it helps us connect to others."[15]

We can age well only if we retain much of our youthful enthusiasm and imagination. People with a young psychology enjoy taking calculated risks and embarking on new adventures. They want freedom from limitations and generally dislike authority. They often make up life as they go along. They can be lovable and, at times, annoying. Being civil and compromising can be challenging for them, so it is best to give the person with a young psychology space and allow them their independent existence. Remember that these youthful figures are a fountain of youth, a source of green immaturity and open-eyed wonder that can keep us hopeful. Without them, we succumb to depressing old age.

How are you aging well? Write down specifics.

As we age, the question of retirement and refocusing can gain more importance and focus. There's a great quote about retirement: "Yesterday a peacock; today a feather duster." Some people choose not to retire until they absolutely must, while others retire as early as possible. The process can and should start many years before we actually retire from our work. Getting ready is important. Replacing work and refocusing our time and energy on something meaningful we can commit to is a critical aspect of aging well.

Retirement generally brings out the contrast between our innermost, best self and our outer self. For many people, their work life and career have been primarily about the outer self—earning money, feeling successful, winning, achieving goals, and gaining prestige. The deeper inner self, which can be called the soul, lives on a vastly different set of values. These can include knowledge, contemplation, deeply felt experiences, meaningful relationships, community, art, beauty, a sense of home, relaxation and comfort, and spiritual peace. Aging well allows us to refocus and retire more engaged than ever, but engaged with things that matter to us and the world. The Taoist ideal can be especially valuable at this stage: *achieve much without doing; doing what you need to do without the old qualities of effort and anxiety.*

In retirement, what can you do to be more engaged than ever? What are you or will you be doing to develop your inner self (even before retirement)?

3

MANAGING OURSELVES

"Never give up then for that is just the place and time that the tide will turn."

Harriet Beecher Stowe

Another critical part of being strong and personally thriving is managing ourselves well in order to create more and better options for ourselves. Managing ourselves well leads to more accomplishment with less stress. It allows us to avoid many potential pitfalls and to make fewer impulsive decisions that don't move us in the direction we wish for ourselves.

We can manage ourselves well by cultivating good habits and routines. Another aspect of managing ourselves well is creating a solid frame of mind. It's also highly valuable to know our skills and talents.

Developing Habits and Routines

"Practice isn't something you do when you're good. It's the thing you do that makes you good." Malcolm Gladwell

Developing good habits is a central part of managing ourselves well and thriving. Some habits are more mundane and straight-forward. For example, we can form a good habit with regard to where we put our wallets and keys when we come home at the end of the day. If we put them in the same place every time, we have no problem locating them quickly the following day. If instead we put them in a different location each time, maybe because we are distracted or because we need to establish a habit, things can get stressful, and we can waste a lot of time. I am highly visual, and the old saying "out of sight, out of mind" is very true for me. As a result, in addition to always putting my wallet and keys in the same place, one habit that helps me a lot is placing things I will need for the next day right near the front door.

I also have a habit of using Post-it notes liberally (including on the inside of the front door). One more habit I appreciate is cleaning our house every Friday afternoon, washing the bathroom and kitchen floors, emptying the trash cans, and using my great vacuuming skills. I also do these tasks the day before we go on vacation so that we return to a clean house. Daily, weekly, and other periodic habits and routines can be enormously helpful!

What good habits and routines do you have that are helpful? What are your bad habits?

An essential habit is to be prepared emotionally, intellectually, and physically. It's helpful to attend meetings, interviews, tests, and outdoor activities well prepared. Physically, we need to take care of ourselves going into stressful situations and in the lead-up to significant challenges. We need to get in proper physical shape to finish the challenge enjoyably. Take the right things—shoes, rain gear, windbreaker, sunblock, plenty of water, and a snack. When your children are in high school, I recommend that you tell them to go to sleep early the night before a major exam or standardized test, then wake up early on test day and take a shower to wake up fully. Prepare a hearty, high-protein breakfast to get them fueled for the day. I also recommend that you take them to school or the exam location, being calm, pleasant, and encouraging. Tell them you believe in them and love them no matter what.

In what ways do you prepare properly? Give examples.

Habits can be enormously valuable in terms of achieving our goals. In Stephen Covey's *The 7 Habits of Highly Effective People*, habits 1, 2, and 3 are about independence and self-mastery:

1. **Be proactive.** Central to this is acting based on chosen values rather than just reacting to external factors or our emotions. This can lead to more meaningful and significant impact.

2. **Begin with the end in mind.** This entails having a clear understanding of the desired outcome and aligning actions to it, whether in a relationship, work project, or life overall.

3. **Put first things first.** This means focusing on essential things by understanding our priorities and saying no to the unimportant, no matter how urgent, and yes to the essential

things. This allows us to avoid wasting time, energy, and resources on things that matter less.[16]

Do you have these three habits? Give specific examples in your personal and work life.

Here are a few other habits I recommend:

- Do a Values Clarification exercise periodically. Take a blank sheet of paper. Along the left margin, write the numbers 1 through 20. Across the top, label columns "Things I love to do"; "When I last did it" (number of days ago; mark an X if it's been longer than 30 days); "Cost involved"; "Can I do this by myself?"; and "Does it require training, a license, etc.?" Feel free to add other columns too. It might not be easy to do this exercise the first few times you try, but stay with it. After you finish, analyze it—what does this tell you? **Are you doing the things you love? In which ways?**

- Write things down. Your goals, your plans, your resolutions for the New Year. Review them periodically during the year. By writing things down, we clarify what we're thinking (and feeling) and have a much better chance of including all elements of what we would like.

- Make lists of things to do. Make a list of annual, monthly, weekly, and daily to-do's. When we do that, there is a much greater chance that we'll actually do most of these things. It's also quite likely that our scheduling of things will improve so that we're not doing five things one week and nothing the next. This will help create schedules, plan workflow, and stage things. Keep in mind that some items need some action before the more complex work can happen later. This kind of planning will also help determine who needs to sign off or buy in to create alignment, and will clarify whether others are required to help.

- Write little (or bigger) notes to yourself. Maybe as you are watching a TV show or movie. Maybe if someone recommends a book. Then take these notes and incorporate them into your longer to-do list, your list of books to read, and other appropriate places. Doing this makes you much more likely to remember (even if you have a good memory like me) and follow through.

- Make an inventory of important things in your life, such as your closest friends and when you last connected with them. Keeping a log of your vacations will also help your favorite memories return to life.

- Make plans for the future. The planning is often the most enjoyable part of the experience. Along with making the to-do lists discussed above, planning helps us align our short-term priorities with our long-term goals.

- Act as if everyone can see what you are doing, and speak as if everyone can hear what you are saying. This is a big part of having integrity.

- Always reply in a timely fashion. This includes thank-you notes, and also acknowledgments of emails and so on. This is true for personal as well as professional things. The quicker we do this, the easier it is to formulate an acceptable reply, whereas if we are late, in some cases our response must be much better, maybe even excellent.

- Set expectations properly. In many cases, we're better off not having expectations at all and simply allowing ourselves to enjoy what actually happens.

- Speak caringly. There's an English proverb "Use soft words and hard arguments." And Washington Irving seems to have agreed: "A sharp tongue is the only edged tool that grows keener with constant use."

In what ways are you following these habits? What other helpful habits do you have?

Creating a Frame of Mind

"Concentration is the secret of strength in politics, in war, in trade—in short, in all management of human affairs." Ralph Waldo Emerson

Creating a frame of mind reflects, in part, how we spend our time and energy, which is central to our lives and is another key to thriving. There are many aspects to this, including concentrating, creating stillness and solitude, being mindful, having resiliency, being patient, being self-reliant, making commitments, experimenting, finishing strong, and recognizing that often less can be more. These are discussed below.

As for thinking and concentrating, it's doubtful that we could get much done without them. Warren Buffett explained this well when he said, "I insist on a lot of time being spent, almost every day, to just sit and think. That is very uncommon in American business. I read and think. So I do more reading and thinking, and make fewer impulse decisions than most people in business." We certainly would be wise to follow Buffett's lead!

Are you making the time to think and concentrate?

Over many decades, I have had the good fortune to have worked with hundreds of smart executives and lawyers. It's been a pleasure to work with very talented and committed people. However, there is often a dark side that pops up. Sometimes someone thinks they are the "smartest person in the room." This rarely works out well for them or the project we're working on. When I was a Scoutmaster, I used to ask my Scouts, "Who is the smartest person the world has ever had?" Frequently, they'd say Einstein or Newton. Then I'd ask them, "Who is smarter—Einstein alone or Einstein with 10 others?" The point is, it's far better not to think of ourselves as the smartest, strongest, or most talented but rather to share our smarts and work with others.

Have you ever worked with someone who felt they were smarter than everyone else? What did you do? How did it work out?

To create a successful frame of mind, a healthy diet of vision, communication, inspiration, and integrity is valuable. Alone, however, they may not be sufficient for effective personal or organizational leadership. Often it might help to add these nutrients: stillness, silence, and solitude.

- **Stillness** helps curb excessive enthusiasm and allows for information to be absorbed.
- **Silence** helps prevent impulsive or unthinking speech. This can be accomplished by both not speaking at all and wisely picking

our words when we do speak. Silence is especially important at these times: when negotiations are going nowhere; when we or someone else is angry; and when we want to learn more.

- **Solitude** also is crucial for self-management. It provides a time of rest, calm, strengthening, and refreshment. And it can cure chronic burnout.

Throughout my adult life, I have benefited tremendously by routinely creating blocks of time to be still and have solitude. I can still vividly recall taking my organizational behavior professor's advice about this. As I was graduating from the MBA program at Stanford and preparing to drive across the country to my job in New York, he encouraged me to go the entire route alone and to relish this significant point in my life. The 10-day trip through Canada along the Trans-Canada Highway was beautiful, of course, but more significantly, it was a time for me to think quietly about my future life, what was important to me, and how I had gotten to that moment. Thank you, Professor Bradford!

Managing ourselves requires us to make decisions big and small. There are many aspects to this. Some people are much more decisive than others. Some people don't hesitate, while others delay and procrastinate. Sometimes we want to continue to gather more information before making a decision. When do we have enough information? Sometimes we're conflicted because each choice seems to lead in directions we're unsure of or uncomfortable with. Or we're worried about how someone will react. Sometimes we can focus; other times, we're distracted. Gridlock and decision paralysis can set in.

It might help to recognize that a decision accomplishes nothing by itself except creating momentum in a particular direction. Deciding to get married, for example, does not create a long and happy marriage; it just sets that possibility in motion. What decisions do is break the gridlock. They focus our energy and build momentum to carry out what the decision implies. So, make a decision, hopefully a well-informed, good one, and then focus on managing the consequences. If we are managing ourselves well, we are making good decisions. Making good decisions is what having wisdom is all about. This is discussed in chapter 14.

A broader view of a frame of mind recognizes that our world is also about our feelings and about whether we're in being or doing mode. Consider this framework that distinguishes between thinking and feeling, and between being and doing.

	Be	**Do**
Think	Inward, contemplative	Active, accomplishing goals, managing and leading
Feel	Receptive, open	Outward, taking others into consideration

In which of the four quadrants are you functioning most often? Is this intentional, or just a matter of habit? In which quadrant would you like to spend more time?

Engaging in mindfulness is valuable, as it has a broad array of psychological, cognitive, and physical benefits. It helps us to see clearly fundamental truths about ourselves and our world so we can make wise choices and respond to life effectively. One specific benefit of mindfulness practice is that it can free us of past conditioning and habitual patterns.

Managing ourselves, as well as other people, also requires a resilient frame of mind. This kind of resiliency encompasses the following: a staunch acceptance of reality; a deep belief, often buttressed by firmly held values, that life is meaningful; and an uncanny ability to improvise. Note that resiliency is also vital to character, as discussed in chapter 1. Organizational and group leadership also requires resiliency. Leadership and management are described in chapter 10.

Another ingredient of managing ourselves well is patience. Leo Tolstoy appropriately addressed patience as critical to self-management when he wrote, "The strongest of all warriors are these two—Time and Patience." We know that everyone thinks about things differently and factors in different things when they make decisions. As a result, some people take a bit longer to think things through. This has often been challenging for me to accept. My wife, for example, takes longer to make decisions than I do because she usually considers how something would get done, not just (like me) whether it's a good idea or whether I'd like to do it. Being patient with her and others has been very helpful!

Managing ourselves well also includes being appropriately self-reliant. Related to being prepared, a habit discussed above, being self-reliant means relying on our own powers and resources rather than those of others. Being self-reliant can be a great virtue. Factoring in everything that matters to you and then making your own decision is something to cherish, not to be farmed out. One of my favorite examples is when we teach someone to drive a car—maybe our son or daughter (as was the case for me). As part of teaching them how to drive, teaching them how to change a tire helps them be self-reliant. Yes, maybe they could get help by calling a roadside service, but if they were out of cell phone range or the roadside truck wouldn't be able to arrive for hours, or maybe waiting didn't feel safe, then being able to change the tire themselves might be quicker and safer.

While getting help from others is often a good thing, being overly dependent on others is likely not a good strategy. People might not help when you need them (as in the example of the flat tire), or their help might not lead us where we hoped it would. A few questions to ask yourself about relying on others: Will there be a time when I really need to know how to do this on my own? Will I give up too much independence and control along the way? Will my values be preserved and my goals met?

Managing ourselves well also means being fully engaged. As Walter Wriston said, "If you miss 7 balls out of 10, you're batting 300, and that's good enough for the Hall of Fame. You can't score if you keep the bat on your shoulder."

Related to being fully engaged is demonstrating commitment, which is high on the list of things we do when managing ourselves well. Here are five levels of commitment I developed years ago. Using this ladder also helps to evaluate and encourage others we work with.

Level 1: I'm not sure if I really want to be here.

Level 2: Maybe I'll try.

Level 3: I'll try when it's convenient for me.

Level 4: I'll definitely try.

Level 5: I'll do whatever it takes.

Are you fully engaged? Which level of commitment are you at most often? How about the people you work with?

Experimenting is another component of managing ourselves well. Sometimes what we are doing isn't working out. We have tried repeatedly, and still it's not working. Now what? Try something new, something different. Think of it as an experiment. And we know that some experiments work and some don't. It's okay; keep going. Keep experimenting.

In some cases, it also helps to follow the "Rhino Principle."[17] When a rhinoceros perceives an object, it makes a quick decision on whether to charge. It puts everything it has into that charge. When the charge is over, the object either is flattened or has fled to cover. That is what the rhino does, and it does it very well.

Success in various fields, such as business, politics, and life in general, often comes from a concentrated pursuit of a central objective. We persistently and repeatedly take action toward achieving this goal, even if it means charging at it again and again. We can learn from the rhino: **to charge!**

Finishing strong is another aspect of managing ourselves well. This is so important that I noted it previously in chapter 1 as one of the key character strengths that lead to life satisfaction and achievement. Sometimes, it is a matter of how we consciously manage ourselves. For example, when we're exhausted or at the end of our rope while working on a project, or as we are leaving one position for another, we might want to wrap up quickly and move on. Be sure as you manage yourself that you finish strong. When we fail to finish strong, we might have to live with regret, and we might burn bridges.

One of the things I like to say is "Less is more." Consider this saying as you manage yourself and make choices about how to spend scarce resources like time and money. Many people and families try to do too much, and as a result, they accomplish less than they'd like.

Trying to do too much can also lead to dissatisfaction and unnecessary stress. Burnout is also a possibility. Alternatively, we can choose to lead quiet lives and get through them without achieving much. But if we want to do the important thing, if we hope to leave a record that will be admired and remembered, we must learn to distinguish between the peripheral and the essential. Greg McKeown discusses this in the excellent book *Essentialism: The Disciplined Pursuit of Less*. It explains how in every aspect of our personal and work lives, what we focus on determines much of what we accomplish and how we feel about it. A must-read!

In what ways are you making choices that reflect "less is more"?

Knowing Our Skills and Talents

"Talent wins games, but teamwork and intelligence win championships." Michael Jordan

What's the difference between talent and skill? Talent is fundamentally something we are born with. Examples are being fast, having excellent eye-hand coordination, and having a great voice. Skill is something that can be taught. Examples of skills include how to code or how to provide excellent customer service. When choosing a job, especially a career, and when pursuing our passions and purpose, we are well advised to consider our skills and talents. Applying this knowledge will help us thrive. In his book *Outliers: The Story of Success*, Malcolm Gladwell has written that we need to accrue 10,000 hours of an activity to achieve a level of excellence.

The following are categories of talent and skills:

Communication—writing, editing, formatting, researching, summarizing, speaking, selling, influencing, translating, interviewing, consulting, promoting, speaking a foreign language

Humanitarian—advising, coaching, counseling, mentoring, motivating, persuading, training, supporting, advocating, explaining, listening, negotiating

Creative—performing, composing, cooking, designing, decorating, inventing, landscaping, painting, sculpting, producing, displaying, craft making, using intuition

Organizational—leading, managing, deciding, delegating, scheduling, supervising, calculating, budgeting, comparing, evaluating, planning, coordinating, implementing, negotiating

Analytical—analyzing, synthesizing, conceptualizing, categorizing, problem-solving, improving, brainstorming, researching, observing, evaluating, visualizing

Technical—repairing; restoring; building; keyboarding; measuring; testing; operating equipment; programming; networking; designing; understanding electronics, schematics, and cartography

Physical—having body coordination, 20/20 vision, acute hearing, eye-hand coordination, finger dexterity, physical strength, flexibility, stamina, sensitivity to touch or smell

Identifying our preferred work environment and preferred time frame for focusing and interacting is also valuable. Consider whether you prefer to work alone or in groups; whether you'd rather work indoors or outdoors, or some combination; and what is the preferred time frame for the work you do—short (maybe less than an hour), days, weeks, or even years (such as for research).

What are your skills? Your talents? What is your preferred environment and work time frame?

Beyond generally knowing your talents and skills, it's also helpful to know if there are things in which you particularly excel and what related aspects of your personality are most valuable.

What are your unique gifts and talents?

4

MONEY

"Yet to have more is not to be more."

Abraham Joshua Heschel

In our world today, handling money and our financial matters well is a critical component of thriving. There are a number of key issues people need to sort out about money. One of the most important is understanding our values and determining how much money we really need. This is a crucial thing to agree on with a partner if you have one. This clarity can lead to many more options and choices in life, and not doing this work can lead to considerable frustration, disappointment, arguments, and worse. Money also plays a significant role in communities and affects our charitable and philanthropic thinking and action.

My wife and I have taken this advice seriously. Our choices reflect our values. We have been budget conscious and have not been excessive in our spending on nonessential things, such as cars, jewelry, and expensive vacations. I have worked hard and have been able to earn enough to live comfortably. Our house is not huge, but we have made it our loving home. I have spent the time to understand investing and have found experienced financial advisors whom I trust, and with whom I can communicate well. We happily invested in our children's college education. We have always made a point to be charitable and philanthropic. We are grateful that making these choices together created a solid foundation for our lives together.

Questions That Shape Our Lives

"Too many people spend money they haven't earned, to buy things they don't want, to impress people they don't like." Will Rogers

The quality of our lives is largely determined by how we decide to spend our time and energy, both of which are more scarce than we might think. As John Levy explained, the type of life we live is heavily influenced by the amount of these limited resources we dedicate to accumulating wealth. We often make decisions regarding the fundamental questions that shape our lives largely based on what we consider to be "enough money." Whatever choice we make comes with specific benefits and requires certain sacrifices. These questions may include the following:

What career will I choose?

How hard will I work?

Where will I live?

What sort of partner will I choose?

How many children will I have?

What kind of lifestyle do I want?

How much money do I want to leave for my children when I die?[18]

Please review the questions above (and many others you may have) and develop your own answers. This may take some time. Don't feel like you need to tackle these questions all at once.

In answering this for ourselves, it's valuable to look at various reasons for having more money than we absolutely need, such as:

Security—protection for oneself and one's family against potential crises, such as sickness, accident, loss of work, and financial downturn

Comfort and pleasure—ways life can be enhanced by having things and experiences beyond the necessities

Prestige—the benefits that come with being admired and respected, though this involves being driven to some degree by the opinions of others

Competitiveness—"Making money is the best game in town."

Philanthropy—being able to support activities that align with our core values and beliefs, and people for whom we are concerned

Power—the capacity to accomplish goals and tasks—for ourselves, our family and friends, our world, or a specific aspect of it

Future generations—the advantage of being able to provide the benefits of affluence to those who come after us

To sort this out entails a fair amount of inner searching. Thriving requires us to be free of what others—parents, other influencers, and media—have tried to convince us of.

What are your reasons for making more money than you need? Whatever you ultimately decide, periodic reexamination is warranted.

It's important to realize that considerable resources are spent every year in our society to convince us that we are "economic animals," meaning that the primary factor, or at least one of the most critical factors, in any decision should be personal economics. This is not true unless you allow it to be. We most definitely are also able to make choices based on our values, our concern for the planet, and our concerns for other people.

How Much Money Is Enough?

"The highest reward for man's toil is not what he gets for it, but what he becomes by it." John Ruskin

An excellent book on the subject of how much money is enough is *Your Money or Your Life: 9 Steps to Transforming Your Relationship with Money and Achieving Financial Independence,* by Vicki Robin and Joe Dominguez. They explain that there are a few consistent qualities in the lives of people who have come to know how much money is enough for them. These qualities include the following:

1. Such people have a sense of purpose larger than their own needs, wants, and desires. Desires are infinite, and as one desire is fulfilled, another emerges. Rather than focusing merely on whims and preferences, focusing on real needs and developing a sense of purpose allows us to direct our attention to those things that will serve our mission.

2. They can account for their money. They know where it comes from and where it goes. We can never have enough if we don't know how much we have. There is a sense of clarity that comes from such precision and truthfulness.

3. They have an internal yardstick for fulfillment. Their sense of "enoughness" isn't based on what others have or don't have. It's based on a capacity to look inside and see if something is really adding to their happiness or if it is just more stuff to store, fix, forget about, and ultimately get rid of.

4. They have a sense of responsibility for the world. This includes understanding how their lives and choices fit into the larger social, environmental, and spiritual scheme of things.

"Enoughness" isn't something to "live up to." It's something to discover through the process of truthful and compassionate living. Accepting what we are leads to contentment, which is the greatest wealth. Through a commitment to restraint and justice, we can heal our lives and be part of healing the world.

As you review the above, which qualities do you have that foster a sense of "enoughness"?

Clearly, money can be enormously important and helpful in building a life for ourselves, our families, and our community. Alas, it can also carry with it many problems and can be harmful.[19] As I see it, some of the positives of money for ourselves and our families include:

- Money is needed and wanted to create a standard of living for ourselves.

- Money can fund communications. Keeping everyone in touch is part of the glue that holds a family together. For individuals and families, this includes phone and Internet access.
- Money can help others in need. When someone is in need, it is vital to understand the nature of the need and how it is best met. Sometimes money is not the only or main answer to the problem. Healthy families commit themselves in monetary and other ways for the long term to their own, one another's, and the family's well-being.
- Money can fund education, which builds values, opportunities, and a sense of belonging. The ideals of justice and compassion are nurtured by education. Being able to hire qualified education resources is important, while in some cases, knowledgeable parents can also teach or serve as tutors.
- Money can be used for family-building efforts. It's important to devote plenty of time and resources (including financial) to learning how to do things, how to manage tasks, and how to build individual and group processes and interpersonal skills.
- Money can create staying power. Extra funds can be critical to achieving goals and long-term vision. Extra funds can help avoid a burden that otherwise could destroy a family. A rainy-day account can be enormously valuable.

In short, without adequate funding, how could the individual and family efforts and activities referred to above, as well as others that promote healthy life, be seriously pursued?

Which elements of money for you or your family are most important?

But of course, there is the other side of the coin too. The *negatives* of money in families include the following:

- Money can shift the focus from people, the heart of families, to material possessions, buildings, etc.
- Money can reduce or eliminate our reliance on each other. With affluence, no one needs to share rides or borrow tools or borrow the proverbial cup of sugar. These types of simple actions can add to the pleasure of being at home and contribute to your family's sense of well-being. It's been said that "the surest way to make life difficult for a child is to make life too easy."
- Money can be used (diverted) to pay for services or staff rather than relying on and building relationships with family members. What builds closer relationships or feels more like friendship: a catered dinner or a potluck? On the other hand, in families, it is wise to sometimes order in or go out to a restaurant and take a break from regular burdens like cooking a big meal.
- Money can create an atmosphere of divisiveness. Affluence can diminish close relationships. Family members need to make every effort to avoid ego, envy, and avarice.

Which aspects of money in your family do you feel are least helpful, even harmful?

The positive and negative aspects of money referred to above apply to communities as well, with a few specific comments: funding for facilities, programming, and the necessary staff to run programs is needed for our community to be able to achieve its mission or possibly even exist. Communication may be by word of mouth, but often there is a cost involved in getting the word out. Funding is also needed for management or process skills, as a lack of them is the number one reason communities fail. I particularly endorse community funds used for creating access for disabled people.

The negatives of money in a community also need to be considered. One age-old community problem is buying a plaque on a wall instead of lending a helping hand. Are people who make donations recognized more than people who volunteer their time? Would more people volunteer their time if there was more public acknowledgment? In addition, money can create accelerated community growth, which can be inundating. Central to all growth-related problems in a community is the simple fact that there will be more people around that other members don't know. Some people think they're in a community, but they're only in proximity. True community requires commitment and openness. It is a willingness to extend ourselves to encounter and know others. Too many people and growing too fast can be a recipe for community breakdown.

In thinking about these positives and negatives, I realize that the best use of money frequently boils down to maintaining balance and building solid relationships with others. This is discussed in chapter 9. By maintaining balance and perspective, the positives of money in families and communities can strongly outweigh the negatives.

Financial Advice

"Today is a gift; that's why it's called the present." Eleanor Roosevelt

Here are some principles and core values that have assisted our family in achieving a level of financial and life success. Following these principles has afforded us many opportunities, helped us avoid many problems, and allowed us to help make this world a better place.

- Be honest in your personal and business life.
- Make sure you can always look yourself in the eye. If you do something you are ashamed or embarrassed about, do not hide—make it right, apologize, and make amends. Get up every morning and look in the mirror and see a happy person without having to avert your eyes, and then set about doing the things you are passionate about.
- Make sure you can always take care of yourself. Do not depend on someone else to support you. Even if you choose not to work, you should have a set of skills that will enable you to support yourself and your dependents should circumstances make it necessary.
- If you choose a job in a field you love, you won't work a day for the rest of your life. So be sure you find a career you like— maybe even one you love. If you feel drawn to public service or a nonprofit organization, pursue it. Don't be afraid to change jobs or careers if you find yourself dissatisfied.
- Do a great job at whatever you decide to do—be it waiting tables or brain surgery.
- Never forget to work hard, but share generously and wisely.
- Follow your dreams. We do not expect you to follow our dreams—either by having the careers or experiences we've had or by living where we've lived. We do hope you find a life that is as satisfying to you as ours have been to us.

- Wealth is about relationships and friends. It is not about dollars and cents.
- Don't ever try to control anyone with money.
- Take a risk on someone or something you believe in. If your gamble does not pay off, walk away with what you've learned.
- Money you have earned is much more satisfying than money you have been given, but you should not feel guilty about the money you inherit or are given by your family. Remember the pleasure it gives us to provide you with certain things. Your obligation is to use it wisely and honorably and not squander it. Our intent is to provide you with a "leg up" in your pursuits, not to eliminate your obligation to become a productive and self-sufficient person. View the distributions you receive as a "hand up" rather than a handout.
- Be generous, but do not give money away because you feel guilty about what you have or to garner kudos or prestige.
- In making a charitable donation, consider doing it anonymously. If you can get a tax benefit from a charitable contribution, that is good, but it should not be the primary motivation for your gifts. Also, don't be content to merely be a charitable check-writer. Don't expect or seek to be at the head table or on the board of directors of the high-profile charities in your community. You will get much more than a tax deduction and a name in the program when you roll up your sleeves and serve people rather than spending your time in committee meetings.
- Prepare a monthly budget. Several good Internet-based tools make this easy. Track your expenditures against your budget. There's a good chance you will buy things you really don't need. Maybe some of these are impulse purchases. Also, create an annual savings target. Part of this might come from a 401(k) or

other retirement plan. In addition, depending on your income, you might be able to save money annually from your after-tax earnings and after benefits have been deducted.

- Start saving early for your children's education. Allow the time value of money to work for you and your children.

- Using a credit card is an extremely expensive form of borrowing. Pay off your credit card balance in full every month.

- If you cannot afford to pay cash for a luxury item (vacation, fancy car, jewelry, etc.), you cannot afford it. Avoid borrowing money for an item you cannot afford.

- If you borrow money (other than for the prudent leverage or tax benefits associated with a mortgage, for example), make repaying the loan your first priority.

- Don't risk what you can't afford to lose. Take some risks, but only with that portion of your investments you can afford to lose.

- Don't try to squeeze the last dollar out of a deal. When you make a deal, neither you nor the person you're dealing with should feel "shafted."

- When making investments, keep it simple. Unless you become a professional in the field, you should avoid complicated investment vehicles. You can make money with your money with a few simple principles. Do not get greedy, and do not believe you can predict the markets. Use common sense to adopt a logical long-term investment philosophy and stick to it, making changes as appropriate as circumstances change (e.g., your age, your need for income, and market forces).

- Don't underestimate the value of objective, professional advice in any phase of your life, including career, investments, and financial and retirement planning.

- If you want to feel successful, count all the things you have that money can't buy.
- There is a Zen quote we encourage you to embrace: "The master in the art of living makes little distinction between his work and his play, his labor and his leisure, his mind and his body, his education and his recreation, his love and his religion. He hardly knows which is which. He simply pursues his vision of excellence in whatever he does, leaving others to decide whether he is working or playing. To him, he's always doing both."

Take time to review these. Which of these do you follow? Which are you not following? What advice would you add?

5

EMOTIONS

"Love the struggle because it makes you appreciate
your accomplishments.
Love challenges because they make you stronger.
Love competition because it makes you better.
Love negative people because they
make you more positive.
Love those who have hurt you because they
teach you forgiveness.
Love fear because it makes you courageous."

Jon Gordon

Our emotions—how we feel—significantly impact our ability to thrive. The good news is that we have enormous power to choose how we feel and how we react. This relates to both positive feelings and negative ones. What we think and feel, we become. Correspondingly, I firmly believe that when we change our hearts and minds, we change the direction of our lives. It is also important to realize that emotions are contagious. They have a huge impact on our work environment, teamwork, family life, relationships of all types, and society as a whole.

In this chapter, I'll comment on the following emotions: happiness, love, trust, empathy and compassion, vulnerability, forgiveness, anger, and fear. The chapter also addresses feelings about dying, as this is a part of life that is often mysterious, challenging, and sometimes painful. The chapter ends with the topic of inner peace.

Emotions Are Life

"Your emotions make you human. Even the unpleasant ones have a purpose. Don't lock them away. If you ignore them, they just get louder and angrier." Sabaa Tahir

What is life without emotions? Emotions equal life. For this reason, when Descartes said, "I think, therefore I am," I believe he had it only partially correct. I think that even more powerful is "I feel, therefore I am."

There is a long list of positive feelings, including acceptance, respect, awe, wonder, joy, happiness, thrill, anticipation, calmness, comfort, contentment, courage, determination, delight, glee, peace, love, gratitude, security, tolerance, and understanding.

And there is a long list of negative feelings, including contempt, bitterness, boredom, apathy, arrogance, avoidance, depression, disgust, disappointment, embarrassment, fear, envy, lust, guilt, hate, impatience, inadequacy, jealousy, negativity, sadness, stress, paranoia, pity, pride, rage, regret, shame, and unhappiness.

To help you understand our emotions and how they are interconnected, I highly recommend reading Chip Conley's book *Emotional Equations: Simple Truths for Creating Happiness + Success.* Among others, he addresses factors and emotions that let us get the most out of life, including curiosity (wonder plus awe), innovation (creativity without cynicism), thriving (the frequency of feeling positive divided by the frequency of feeling negative), self-esteem (success divided by pretentiousness), calling (pleasure divided by pain), and flow (your skill divided by the challenge you face).[20]

Happiness

"Happiness is a how, not a what; a talent, not an object."
Hermann Hesse

Happiness has been studied and written about extensively over the millennia. There is quite a range of thoughts about what produces happiness, some of which are discussed below.

Studies show that longevity and health correlate with happiness. Research has also shown that our own happiness is based on the following: 50 percent is from our natural set point; 10 percent is from life circumstances (good or bad), from which the resulting happiness only lasts approximately 90 days, and then we return to our set point; and the remaining 40 percent is based on intentional activity, which includes the choices we make and finding meaning in our lives. Because of how large a percentage—40 percent—of our happiness is based on intentional activity, it's easy to conclude that most people are about as happy as they make up their minds to be.

Some people think happiness is about relationships with others. They believe relationships, especially romantic relationships, are one of the most significant factors in happiness. Others believe there is tremendous happiness in making others happy despite their own situation. If we share whatever happiness we experience with others, we will multiply the happiness that comes into our lives. There's a great saying, "Shared grief is half the sorrow, but happiness, when shared, is doubled." And the Buddha said, "Thousands of candles can be lighted from a single candle, and the life of the candle will not be shortened. Happiness never decreases by being shared. Unlike material possessions, which are usually finite, happiness is infinite."

For me personally, I am happiest when I am "invisible," when I am not focusing on myself but on another person or a project I am committed to. I also find great pleasure in a hard day of honest physical work. At these times, when I put my head on the pillow, sleep comes peacefully.

Who is the happiest person you know? What are they doing to be happy? What priority are they making in their relationships?

Having lots of experiences is another avenue people speak about as a source of happiness. They fill their lives with as many moments and experiences of joy and passion as they humanly can. They start with one experience and build on it. In terms of having lots of experiences, research shows that people report that the best part of their vacation is planning for it; the reality of the vacation isn't always as happy. So, plan your vacation and then be flexible, go with the flow, and have humor.

And it can certainly be argued that it's the simple things in life that make us happy—a smile, a word of praise, a moment of shared laughter, a helping hand, a caring heart. Happy people slow things down. And they breathe. We are most alive and happiest in those moments when our hearts are conscious of these simple treasures.

From my experiences in life, I'm pretty sure that the key to happiness and success is being thankful for the gifts we have received and being optimistic and excited about the new gifts coming our way. I love the saying "Abundance will flow into our life when gratitude flows out of our heart."

What leads to your happiness?

Professor Fred Luskin[21] says that happiness is a life experiment for ourselves. Many people cannot see what's good about themselves and the world because it's hard to analyze our own data. His studies show that the happiest people are acultural and are not concerned about fitting in. They are inner-directed and have a powerful purpose. The two main obstacles to happiness are cultural: trying to fit into norms and fear of being unworthy or not having enough.

Luskin argues that it helps to apply Maslow's hierarchy of needs[22] in assessing happiness. This reveals the following (in order of the most basic to the most high-level needs in the hierarchy):

Physiological and Safety Needs: Once we have enough (approximately $75,000 a year in income), earning more doesn't add much to our happiness. People concentrate too much on material things—a bigger house, a fancier car—at the expense of happiness. There is a Buddhist saying, "The source of unhappiness is wanting things. To be happy, want nothing."

Love and Belonging Needs: The core of this is being able to give and receive love. This takes a commitment of time to do; it helps us to reflect on what's important. To be happy, we have to create pathways and practice.

Esteem Needs: The average middle-class American spends 70 to 80 percent of their time complaining. We have a hardwired negativity bias. Our nervous system will fixate on risks everywhere, looking for what's wrong and what doesn't work. To overcome this, we have to choose happiness and take charge. To be happy, we have to feel good about our contributions.

Self-Actualization Needs: We need to ask ourselves, "Did I take my unique gifts and take risks to offer them?" Happiness is best without mediators, such as success and status, but rather, directly. Happiness grows best from involvement in valued activities and progress toward one's goals, and far less from passive experiences, even of desirable circumstances. To be happy and to self-actualize, make peace with life. Be grateful. Appreciate beauty, wisdom, and goodness—they're all around if we only take the time to look.

Carl Jung[23], who founded analytical psychology, believed that deep happiness is possible, but not without cost. He believed that sometimes happiness surges from the deepest suffering. He counseled that we must not avoid suffering. When we distance ourselves too much from suffering, we lose depth, which is where happiness comes from. It also seems that chasing happiness can make us miserable. And if we consider what it takes to be unhappy, think about how correlated unhappiness is to being self-centered.

With all these perspectives about happiness in mind, we can see that there are many things in our control and choices we can make in order to be happier.

What can you do to be happier? What choices can you make?

Here's some advice from experts on obtaining happiness:[24]

Relish the day. When you experience something positive, find a way to prolong the feeling. Celebrate the small things, not just the big ones. For example, you might celebrate even modest career accomplishments. Or when you're on vacation, take photos and purchase souvenirs so you remember the trip longer.

Avoid lack of control. The feeling of being out of control often leads to stress. Studies show that commuting ranks as one of life's least enjoyable and often very stressful activities. So, among other things that produce stress, avoid traffic and long lines.

Stop worrying, especially about things you have no control over.

In every life we have some trouble
But when you worry, you make it double.
Don't worry, be happy. Bobby McFerrin

See friends and family, as this produces some of our happiest times, especially in the right amounts, venues, and activities.

Spend your time well. We can boost our level of happiness by thinking carefully about how we spend our time. Try buying memorable experiences, such as going to a favorite restaurant or on a trip. Enjoy the anticipation leading up to it and follow the first tip above (relish the day) afterward.

Limit options. Having lots of choices can lead to dissatisfaction. When given a choice, such as an option to return a purchase, the mind becomes conflicted with indecision. When options are closed, the mind experiences a sense of contentment.

When we get excited about life, we get an exciting life.

Here are a few happiness exercises. Before these exercises, take several deep breaths into your abdomen. Slow down. Then, ask yourself:

In the past 72 hours, who has been kind to me? What's been given to me?

Whom do I like and respect? Who has encouraged me for being me and for the qualities I have?

Picture the person you adore. Feel it in your heart.

Associated with happiness, but distinct from happiness, is having fun. As Dr. Seuss wrote in one of my favorite children's books, *The Cat in the Hat*, "It's fun to have fun, but you have to know how."

What's the difference for us between fun and entertainment? Between doing something exciting and doing something enjoyable? I like this line from the movie *State and Main*: "Everyone makes their own fun. If you don't make it yourself, it isn't fun, it's entertainment." With this definition of fun in mind, to have more fun on a more regular basis, try these exercises:

Exercise 1: Write down what you do for *fun*. The clearer you are about this, the more likely you'll be able to make it happen.

Exercise 2: What did you do for fun in the past three months? Write it down, or better yet, share this with a friend. Make the experiences come back alive. Be specific (who, what, when, where). How did you feel?

Exercise 3: What are you planning (or hoping) to do in the next three months that you expect and hope will be fun? Again, write this down or share it with a friend.

Love

"Love is the river of life in this world." Henry Ward Beecher

Love is the subject of a vast number of books, movies, and songs. In our culture and media, most love is romantic love, conditional love. We use expressions like *finding true love, love at first sight, I love you*, and *you love me*. We see love as waiting to be found, grasped, or fallen into or out of. But the truth is, we can't get love from anybody, and we can't give love to anybody.[25] We are love (or, sadly, we're not).

The type of love that is commonly recognized and praised in our society is not the universal kind that connects us all. Krista Tippett, who hosts the podcast *On Being*, wrote the following about love: "We've made it private, contained it in the family, when its audacity is in its potential to cross tribal lines. We've fetishized it as romance, when its true measure is in a quality of sustained, practical care. We've lived it as a feeling, when it is a way of being."[26]

Love is the only thing grand enough to encompass the vastness of human society and the difficulties of the current times. With this in mind, Tippett went on to say, "It is time to dare this more bravely in our midst and dare learning together how love can be practical, creative, and sustained as a social good, not merely as a private good."[27]

The more open we are, the more we receive love. And the love we withhold is the only source of pain we have when we die. I have pledged to start telling people more often what I love about them so that they hear this while I am still living.

Are you living love as a way of being? Give specific examples. What more can you be doing?

Studies have shown that there are five "languages" of love. This concept may have originated with Gary Chapman.[28] People almost always have one primary language of love. Often in love relationships, each of the two partners has a different language of love; often, the other partner isn't aware of the language being spoken by their partner. This can lead to confusion and potentially significant relationship problems. The five languages of love are:

- Words (for example, saying, "I love you")
- Being physical, including touch, hugging, and sexual relations
- Service—doing something for the other person they prefer not to do themselves (e.g., getting the car serviced regularly)
- Physical gifts
- Organizing quality time together

What is your primary language of love? Your loved ones'? What can you do to better respond to your loved ones' languages of love?

Many parents say that their love for their children is more important than anything else in their lives. Yet parents often have to say or do things that make their kids think they are "unloved." Sometimes it takes significant courage to show your love. Here are a few cases. They all begin with "I loved you enough to . . ."

- make you return a Milky Way bar with a bite out of it to the store and confess that you didn't pay for it.
- insist that you buy a bike with your own money, even though we could afford it.
- ignore what "everyone else's" mother or father said or did.
- ask where you were going, with whom, and when you'd be home.
- let you assume your own responsibilities at ages 6, 10, and 16.
- accept you for the person you are, not for the person I wanted you to be.
- admit I was wrong and ask you to forgive me.

Most of all, I loved you enough to say no when you hated me for it. That was the hardest part of all.

In what ways are you showing your love for your children?

Trust

"I'm thankful for all the times when my trust was greater than my fear." Author unknown

Like so many other emotions, trust starts with ourselves. Trust that we will find our way. Trust that we will come to a time when holding on hurts more than letting go. Choose to have your trust be greater than your fears, real or imagined.

In these ways, do you trust yourself?

Multiple types of trust show up in different relationships, between partners, within families, and at the workplace. These include:

Trust that you'll follow through—Being dependable

Trust that you'll do as you say—Keeping your word

Trust that you'll make good decisions—Having good judgment, being financially prudent

Trust that you'll communicate with me and include me

Trusting you with my feelings—Are you oblivious to my feelings? Do you know them? Do you ask? Do you care? Do you ignore my feelings? Do you intentionally hurt my feelings?

Trust that you will not hurt me physically or emotionally

Trust that you will understand that there are times when I feel very differently about something than you do

In which ways are you trustworthy? What can you do to be more trustworthy?

The number one issue in marriages is trust and betrayal. I feel hugely fortunate that trust has been the foundation of my long and strong marriage. According to John Gottman,[29] one of the foremost relationship experts in the United States, key questions include:

- Can I trust you to be present and listen to me when I'm distressed?
- Can I trust you to prioritize me over your family and friends?
- Can I trust you to be sexually faithful and not cheat on me?
- Can I trust that you will show me respect?
- Can I trust that you will assist me with household tasks?
- Can I trust you to actively participate in parenting our children?

The most desirable qualities in a partner are dependability, honesty, and the ability to build trust. A graduate student of John Gottman, Dan Yoshimoto, developed the acronym **ATTUNE**:

A—**A**wareness of your partner's emotions

T—**T**urning toward the emotion

T—**T**olerance for two different viewpoints

U—trying to **U**nderstand your partner

N—giving **N**ondefensive responses

E—responding with **E**mpathy

How strong is the mutual trust between you and your partner? Are you ATTUNEd?

Empathy and Compassion

"Compassion is a language the deaf can hear and the blind can see." Mark Twain

What's the difference between empathy and compassion? Empathy refers to our ability to understand and feel another person's emotions. Compassion occurs when those feelings and thoughts include the desire to help.

Empathy includes putting ourselves in another person's place as if we were feeling those feelings. There are three main types of empathy: cognitive, emotional, and compassionate. At its core, cognitive empathy is more rational and logical. It requires us to look at the situation or person from a perspective that might be foreign to us. To have cognitive empathy, we have to factor in our own biases and our history and values as we listen to another. We need to understand that we often see things only as we want them to be and not as they really are; that there's a blurry line separating honesty and judgment.

In the second form of empathy, emotional empathy, we literally feel the other person's emotions. An example would be a mother smiling at her baby and the baby smiling back. It's like "catching" the emotion.

And the third variety, compassionate empathy, is what we usually understand as empathy—feeling someone else's pain and taking action to help. This requires respect for another person. It includes tolerating and accommodating. Like sympathy, compassion is about concern for someone but with an additional move toward action to mitigate the problem. Lloyd Shearer spoke eloquently about compassion when he said, "Resolve to be tender with the young, compassionate with the aged, sympathetic with the striving, and tolerant of the weak and the wrong. Someday in life you will have been all three."

Generally, people who want or need our empathy don't just need us to understand (cognitive empathy, which is underemotional), and they certainly don't need us to feel their pain or, worse, to burst into tears alongside them (emotional empathy, which can be overemotional). Instead, they need us to understand and sympathize with what they are going through and then crucially either take or help them take action to resolve the problem. This is compassionate empathy and is the balance between logic and emotion. This balance is vital, for as Albert Schweitzer said, "Until he extends his circle of compassion to all living things, man will not find peace."

In my career, I have benefited by having cognitive empathy. However, in my personal relationships, especially with my family,

I recognized the need to have more compassionate empathy. Thankfully, with work and focus, I am much more able to have this type of empathy now and be more compassionate.

Which type or types of empathy do you have? Give examples of how you have been compassionate.

Vulnerability

"People are like stained glass windows. They sparkle and shine when the sun is out, but when darkness sets in their true beauty is revealed only if there is a light from within." Elisabeth Kübler-Ross

If we are disconnected from love (of ourselves or others), we can feel shame that we're not good enough. The essence of this is feeling vulnerable. We often then try to become more certain and less flexible and work on trying to be perfect. The coping mechanism for vulnerability is to numb vulnerability. Since we can't selectively numb, feelings of joy, happiness, and gratitude are all numbed as well.

It is common to view vulnerability as a form of weakness, but there's a type of vulnerability that shows our strength and presence. When we establish genuine connections with others, we can experience love and a sense of belonging. We believe we're worthy just as we are. This is the essence of being "wholehearted," as explained in a wonderful TED Talk by Brené Brown. Being wholehearted requires us to be vulnerable, to have the courage to acknowledge our imperfections and allow our true selves to be seen. We relinquish control and welcome our vulnerability. This process creates a feeling of "I am enough," which can result in becoming authentic (who a person really is). People who fully embrace their vulnerability and become wholehearted realize that their vulnerability makes them beautiful and attractive to others. [30]

Are you feeling vulnerable? Wholehearted? What experiences have you had when your vulnerability showed your strength and presence?

Forgiveness

"Forgiveness does not change the past, but it does enlarge the future." Paul Boese

Sometimes people need to actively forgive themselves or others before they can let go and be present. If we can't forgive, we can't heal. When we let go of hurt and forgive, we grow. As Miguel Ruiz wrote, "The supreme act of forgiveness is when you can forgive yourself for all the wounds you've created in your own life. Forgiveness is an act of self-love. When you forgive yourself, self-acceptance begins as self-love grows." But sometimes we're not ready to let go and forgive. We have to trust our own timing. We have to forgive ourselves for not being ready—yet.

What usually blocks forgiveness is pride and resentment. Sometimes forgiveness is blocked by an unwillingness to accept the past. Rev. Don Felt wisely said, "Forgiveness means giving up all hope for a better past." Nelson Mandela knew this as he left prison after 27 years. He knew that if he didn't leave his bitterness and hatred behind, he'd still be in prison—the prison of his own mind. And yet, while it's important to forgive, we should not forget. We don't want the same thing to happen again.

There might be different things we have or haven't done to someone else for which we'd like to be forgiven. These include:

- Something we have done that was hurtful, whether intended or not
- Not giving another person what they need or not being supportive of them
- Not knowing or checking with another person about what they need

What would you like to be forgiven for?

If someone comes to us and sincerely asks for forgiveness, we can choose to open our hearts and accept their apology. And when asking another person to forgive us for something we have done, we can at least forgive ourselves if they continue to refuse to forgive us.

Consider these five steps of repentance:

1. Recognize and discontinue the improper action. This involves knowing that certain actions are more than just lapses. We have to analyze our motives deeply.
2. Verbally confess the action, thus giving the action a concrete form in your own mind. This involves declaring and acknowledging the action openly and admitting you did it.
3. Regret the action. Evaluate the negative impact this action may have had on you and others. This includes feelings of regret for failing to maintain your moral standards.

4. Determine never to repeat the action. Picture a better way to handle it.

5. Make restitution where possible. This is the act of making good, as best one can, for any damage done. Personal Note: I hope we can develop a more robust system of restorative justice, a system of criminal justice that focuses on rehabilitating offenders through reconciliation with victims and the community at large.

From whom do you want to ask forgiveness? For what?

Emotional Upset or Anger

"There are a few things that make me angry. Mostly things not going my way." Sebastian Vettel

A wide range of feelings is associated with being upset when we struggle with difficult relationships or situations. In the book *Emotional Equations*, Conley discusses feelings of anger or being upset, including despair, disappointment, regret, jealousy, envy, anxiety, humiliation, suffering, remorse, and workaholism. If any of these are active in your life, I highly recommend reading this book!

I've read that most people live with one of two mindsets, which have enormous implications for how people feel and behave. Often these lead to negative feelings. These mindsets are:

- **Everyone is out to get me.** How do you respond if you have this mindset? Are you blaming others for things that are happening to you? Consider this bumper sticker: "I was having a bad day until I figured out who to blame it on."

- **I know better.** This can include being committed to being right, being in command, or being the authority. If you have this mindset, what does this lead to? How does it affect your relationships with others? Are you able to listen?

Do you live with one of these mindsets? Give examples.

When thinking about negative emotions, the following Twelve Steps to Insanity,[31] while a bit tongue-in-cheek, are worthy of consideration:

1. We admitted we were powerless over nothing—that we could manage our lives perfectly. We could also perfectly manage the lives of those around us.
2. We came to believe that there was no greater power than ourselves and that the rest of the world was insane.
3. We made a decision to have our loved ones turn their wills and lives over to our care even though they couldn't understand us at all.
4. We made a searching and fearless inventory of everyone we knew.
5. We admitted to the whole world the exact nature of everyone else's wrongs.
6. We were entirely ready to make them give us the respect we thought we deserved.
7. We demanded that others do our will because we were always enlightened.
8. We made a list of all the persons who had harmed us and became willing to go to any length to get even with them all.
9. We got direct revenge on such people wherever possible except when to do so would cost us our lives or at least a jail sentence.

10. We continued to take inventory of others, and when they were wrong, promptly and repeatedly told them about it.

11. We sought through complaining and self-medication to improve our relations with others as we could not understand them at all, asking only that they do things our way.

12. Having had a complete physical, emotional, and spiritual breakdown as a result of these steps, we tried to blame others and get sympathy in all our affairs.

Do any of these sound familiar?

What can you do when you have negative feelings? When you get angry or upset, it will help to sort out why. You need to calm down to see things more clearly. Was it because of something you wanted and didn't get? Was it because of something someone said or didn't say? Was it because someone did or didn't do what you felt they should or shouldn't have done (or you would have or wouldn't have done)? Was it something else?

Which negative emotions do you feel? Dial into specific memories and experiences. How are they limiting your life today? What can you do to change?

Along my journey, I have felt upset or even angry more times than I care to remember. Often, the most difficult times for me are when I feel confused about how I am feeling because how I am feeling is complex. It's not just one emotion, even a strong one—it's a layering and weave of interrelated emotions and even multiple experiences all thrown together. To make progress, I need to take the time to sort out these various feelings. Only then can I determine a course of action. I've realized that we can't let go of anything if we don't open to acceptance—of ourselves, of others, of the circumstances.

For me, keeping a journal is very beneficial. Journaling allows me to understand my feelings by breaking confusing and multiple feelings into parts. This helps give me perspective as well as the critical space between the source of the problem (the stimulus) and my response. In this space is the ability to choose my response. I know that in my response is my opportunity for growth. This is power that can help me move from feelings of darkness to feelings of light, from negative feelings and a sense of powerlessness to positive feelings, where I have choice and power. And this is when I very much appreciate Hafiz's quote "I wish I could show you, when you are lonely or in darkness, the astonishing light of your own being." However, if the anger or degree of emotional upset is extreme, it could be harmful to us or others, and outside intervention might be called for.

How do you sort through your emotions, especially when they're complicated or upsetting? Do you think you do a good, average, or poor job? What could you do to become better at sorting through your emotions?

Feelings of being upset often stand in the way of our thriving. Beyond sorting them out, I'm sure we'd like to do something constructive about them and look for ways to avoid having those feelings on a regular basis. Suppose you are feeling angry or upset or really any of the negative emotions. In that case, I urge you to take a breath and avoid doing something permanently stupid because you're temporarily upset.

Fear

"May your choices reflect your hopes, not your fears." Nelson Mandela

Fear is a very potent negative emotion. It is a deeply conditioned, automatic reaction to any feeling of being physically or emotionally unsafe. Fear arises uninvited. At times it believes it is protecting you, and occasionally it is. But far more often, it is based on imagined things or imagined selves to be defeated. It is thought that what we most fear has already happened. I appreciate Valarie Kaur's words "What if this darkness you feel is not the darkness of the tomb, but the darkness of the womb? . . . Breathe and then push."

We all have weaknesses. If we are afraid of them and try to cover them up, we probably put ourselves in a situation of having to do more of what we aren't good at and risk making more mistakes. So, when an inkling of fear arises, it's best to acknowledge it. We must not suppress fear. Quite the opposite, we must allow the fear to present itself unimpeded in order to investigate it in its natural environment. Then note it as "fear." If you notice your mind dwelling on it, spinning out its infernal saga, note this as "fearing." It's important to understand that dwelling on a fear won't make it go away. Dwelling on fear is tantamount to bondage.

According to Patrick Lencioni, there are three primary fears:

Fear of Losing

This leads to avoiding difficult decisions and shirking responsibilities. It undermines trust and loyalty. Know that people can smell fear. The healthy response: Speak honestly in a gentle manner. Prioritize providing advice and guidance over selling. Be willing to take calculated and well-thought-out risks. Be prepared to let go of the thing you are striving for if necessary.

Fear of Being Embarrassed

Pride can prevent people from seeking clarification or further information for fear that they'll appear uninformed or foolish. For a strong relationship to develop, both parties must be willing to be vulnerable, experiment, make mistakes, share ideas that might be stupid, and admit errors. The healthy response: Ask seemingly simple, trivial questions. Make dumb suggestions. Acknowledge and salute your mistakes.

Fear of Feeling Inferior

Pride based on the need for a sense of importance and social standing relative to others fuels fears of being inferior. The healthy response: Direct your attention toward the other person rather than yourself. Show respect and appreciation for the other person's work. Be of service by assisting the other person in making improvements, and be ready and willing to undertake tasks others are not willing to do.[32]

And there's more bad news: many times, we don't allow ourselves to love because of fear—fear of being vulnerable, fear that people will not love us back, fear of being left alone. Even love, when it is conditional, can create fear. We need to overcome this kind of fear so that we can love. As Ram Dass and Mirabai Bush observe in their powerful book *Walking Each Other Home: Conversations on Loving and Dying*, "Love can break your heart, but it can also heal your heart."[33] Love is the antidote to fear. It is always available, and it's limitless.

What fears do you have? What are you doing to address them?

Feelings about Dying

"You don't get to choose how you're going to die. Or when. You can only decide how you are going to live. Now." Joan Baez

In the course of life, death visits us frequently in the form of endings and failure. Our lives will be filled with people dying—people we know, have cared for, and have loved. Yet, every time we think of them, they're with us. As discussed in *Walking Each Other Home*, death is the end of the body, not the soul.[34] (Note: Some people don't believe in a soul but in personhood or a life spark. When the word *soul* is used here, feel free to substitute another term that resonates with you.) The soul is eternal, and loved ones who have passed away remain present in a different form. Death may terminate a person's physical existence, but it does not end the bond and connection with our loved ones; instead, it's an "invitation to form a new relationship—soul to soul." When we are ready, we realize that love persists and that the people we have ever loved remain part of the fabric of our being now.

In Western culture, we spend our lives rejecting the process of getting older and the inevitable end of life. Yet the key to dying is the same as the key to living, which is to exist fully in the present moment.[35] I like Treya Wilber's quote "Because I can no longer ignore death, I pay more attention to life." Life is not about longevity as much as it is about intensity. To age well involves accepting the inevitability of death and integrating it into the flow of our life. We age well when we are so familiar with the dynamics of dying that we aren't alarmed by the indications of actual death through illness and the advancement of years.

There are different cultural traditions about the body and death. Nonetheless, when someone is approaching the end of their life, it's important for us to be fully present, listening for what is needed with love and kindness, without imposing our ideas or expectations of how they should die.[36] In this way, as explained in *Walking Each Other Home*, we need to be a "loving rock." The most important thing is to hold the person in our hearts with love. And remember that a soul's departure from the physical realm is precisely timed, occurring neither too early nor too late. For many of us, this may be hard to accept.

As Stephen Levine points out in *A Year to Live: How to Live This Year As If It Were Your Last*, the last year of our life, or that of a person we care deeply about, need not be a morbid process but can be one of acceptance.[37] Undertaking these approaches might help:

- Start paying attention to the things that obstruct the heart and cloud the mind, as well as those that bring clarity and remove obstacles.

- Integrate your insights and prompt the weary mind to rest in an expansive heart.

- Begin experiencing life directly, by savoring the taste of your food rather than contemplating it, actively listening to music instead of simply humming along, and observing new people without making quick judgments or assumptions about them.

- When communicating with others, stay mindful that fear can limit openness and self-awareness, and can hinder the resolution of unresolved issues.
- Remember that love is the most valuable gift one can give.

We need not die defeated by death or have feelings of disappointment, failure, or remorse. Quite the reverse. It is possible to die at peace, with minimal pain, continuing to learn, feeling grateful, and allowing our soul to grow. Dying is a window of opportunity. When Aldous Huxley[38] died, he said, "My goodness, look at that! Extraordinary!" When Steve Jobs[39] died, he said, "Wow!"

What would you do if you knew you had only a year to live? How will you be present when a person you love is dying?

This final year of life can be a time to focus on finishing things before passing away, rather than actively seeking death. During this final year, as Stephen and Ondrea Levine suggest in their book *Who Dies? An Investigation of Conscious Living and Conscious Dying*, it is possible to finish the business of your relationships and to die without regrets. The Levines recommend imagining that you are lying on your deathbed, and the faces of loved ones are looking with concern at you. You want to say farewell, tie up loose ends, and finish your business, to cut through years of incomplete communication. What would you say? Reflect on what has remained unsaid and share that each day with those you love. Don't hesitate. Tomorrow may be too far away.[40]

Finishing business involves opening our hearts, that we let go of whatever blocks our hearts with resentment or fear and whatever we still want from others, and that we simply send love. Finishing business does not necessarily mean we clear up a lifetime of broken communication and lack of trust. This last year can be an opening to go beyond the need to settle accounts. Instead, we can let go of what obstructs our deepest sharing. To finish our business, we must begin to stop holding back. This involves accepting the people who are close to us and matter the most just as they are, without trying to mold them into what we want them to be or who we wish ourselves to be.[41]

Finishing business, even in relationships filled with love, requires us to go beyond emotions. As the Levines point out, when we say love, we are typically referring to an emotion, some deep feeling that momentarily allows us to open to another person. But be aware that in this type of emotional love, the instinct to protect ourself is never too far away. Instead of love being an emotion, it can be a state of being. In this state, it's much more than the absence of anger, fear, doubt, or confusion. It can be a state in which there's no pulling or pushing. By finishing business and being in a state of love, we can greet every moment with compassion rather than fear, and respond to agitation and grief with tranquility and calmness.[42]

Day of the Dead (Día de los Muertos—Mexico)

On the Day of the Dead,
Remember our loved ones.
We remember their love,
We remember their faces,
We remember their voice.

On the Day of the Dead,

We don't get all upset

Because we remember

With joy, not with regret.

We celebrate with flowers and food

With music and tunes

We dance and we sing

On the Day of the Dead

Our hearts will rejoice.

Inner Peace

"Every breath we take, every step we make, can be filled with peace, joy, and serenity." Thich Nhat Hanh

Given the wide range of emotions we feel, both positive and negative, as we live and as we or the ones we love approach death and die, I'd like to end this chapter on emotions with a list by Saskia Davis entitled "The Symptoms of Inner Peace":

1. A tendency to think and act spontaneously rather than from fears based on past experiences
2. An unmistakable ability to enjoy each moment
3. A loss of interest in judging oneself
4. A loss of interest in judging other people
5. A loss of interest in conflict
6. A loss of interest in interpreting the actions of others
7. A loss of ability to worry (Note: This is a very serious symptom of inner peace.)

8. Frequent, overwhelming episodes of appreciation
9. Contented feelings of connectedness with others and nature
10. Frequent attacks of smiling through the eyes of the heart
11. Increasing susceptibility to love extended by others as well as the uncontrollable urge to extend it
12. An increasing tendency to let things happen rather than to make them happen[43]

Do you feel you have inner peace? Which of these symptoms describe you? If not, what is your plan for getting there?

6

SPIRITUALITY AND RELIGION

"Engage in a spiritual life, a life of service and a life of healing: to resist the impulse to shy away from difficulty, suffering, and the grotesque, but instead to cultivate an eye for beauty, a curious mind, and a fearless heart."

Maggid Jhos Singer

Many people say that they are spiritual but not religious. I also understand that some people may be religious but not necessarily spiritual. We are among the first peoples in human history who do not broadly inherit religious identity as a given, a matter of family and tribe. Recent surveys indicate that approximately 30 percent of US adults are religiously unaffiliated. Yet our spiritual and religious traditions are important, as they have carried virtues across time. They give life meaning and help us make the mundane aspects of life sacred. Separately or in some combination we choose, they are an essential part of our tool kit for the art of living. They are a key aspect of thriving in life.

What is the difference between being spiritual and being religious? Spirituality deals with the soul, the self, and our life force. It embodies being openhearted, curious, and humble. Religion is about beliefs, practices, obligations, and community. It often involves conformity. Religion is associated with answers and certainties, while spirituality is about asking searching questions that often elude answers.

Being part of a community is one of the differences between spirituality and religion. While spirituality can be a solo enterprise, religion implies belonging to a community, which can, in many cases, be good and healthy and a source of friendships. The adage holds—when you belong to it, it belongs to you.

I feel very thankful for being both spiritual and religious. I am fundamentally spiritual first, but I also appreciate how practicing a religion of my own has numerous benefits. Elements of both of these are described below.

A Spiritual Life of One's Own

"Our spiritual life is our own—on our lips and in our hearts."
Krista Tippett

There are many ways we can be spiritual and have a sense of awe and wonder be infused in our lives. Being spiritual means being concerned with all of humanity and life, and it involves the appreciation of life's wonders and mysteries. Our spirituality allows us to wander across boundaries of belief and nonbelief, as well as the boundaries of science and faith, which can help us understand our own truths while honoring the reality of the other. Being spiritual can lead us to find inner peace.

Spiritual endeavor is part discipline and part being in awe. Choosing to live a spiritual life of discipline, law, and control can be immensely helpful in facing the challenges we inevitably encounter in life. But to do so, we must wake up, find our own portals to wonder, and go beyond the limits of ordinary experience.

Without spiritual integrity, we risk faking our way through life. We risk clinging to stuff, habits, places, or harmful aspects of the past. We might pretend to have feelings we don't have. We might strive for dominance or maybe do the opposite—hide. We can become self-righteous, or we might conform. And without spirituality, it is easy to bow down to idols of wealth, power, and privilege. "Short is the way from need to greed," as Rabbi Abraham Joshua Heschel said.[44] In order to return to the essence of our own spirit, we need to strip away the external.

Spirituality is persisting in the presence of doubt or confusion so that we are connected to the universal. Consider Gopi Kallayil's metaphor: Think of yourself as an ice cube with your own distinctive shape, color, temperature, and texture. But if you're dropped into the ocean, your limited identity as an ice cube disappears, and you merge into the vastness, becoming one with the sea, your iciness gone, but your essence still there.

The shift to the sacred dimension occurs when we begin to acknowledge others and respond to their needs regardless of personal expediency. This can happen as a result of various events, such as observing other people's suffering, being in love (and better yet, just being love), or being morally educated. A spiritual and religious practice can help us make this life-affirming shift.

In what ways are you spiritual? How does being spiritual help you? What shifts have you already made to become more spiritual? What further shifts can you make?

We can find spiritual nourishment in many ways and places—in service, in literature, in the arts, through meditation and mindfulness practices, through yoga, through music, and in nature, among others. I think Gertrude Stein spoke well of feeling spiritual when she said, "Every day is a renewal, every morning the daily miracle. This joy you feel is life."

To connect with your spiritual self, go out into nature and just lie down on the ground or sit by a river. The running water keeps washing the mind as you watch leaves float down the river. After some time, your mind becomes less confused and cloudy so that you can better see and deeply appreciate things as they are. As the Buddha said, "How wonderful! How wonderful! All things are perfect. Exactly as they are!"

And as we strive to be connected, spirituality can help us recognize that both love and true friendship are more than a way of knowing that we matter to someone else. They are a way of mattering to the world, bringing God into a world that would otherwise be a hollow experience of selfishness and loneliness. The philosopher Martin Buber responded to the question "Where is God?" by answering, "God is found in relationships. God is not found in people; God is found between people. When you and I are truly attuned to each other, God comes down and fills the space between us so that we are connected and not separated."[45]

To begin, take a moment to breathe; be present in the moment; trust the universe to spin without you for a moment. And for a moment, love the life you have been lent. Thich Nhat Hanh, the Vietnamese Buddhist monk, wrote, "Breathing in, I calm my body. Breathing out, I smile. Dwelling in the present moment, I know this is a wonderful moment!"

Where do you find spiritual nourishment? Which relationships do you have in which you are truly attuned to the other person?

A Religion of One's Own

"The fruit of silence is prayer, the fruit of prayer is faith, the fruit of faith is love, the fruit of love is service, the fruit of service is peace." Mother Teresa

Practicing a religion can help us treat with great respect and make sacred so many things in life that would otherwise be ordinary and mundane. In his book *A Religion of One's Own: A Guide to Creating a Personal Spirituality in a Secular World*, Thomas Moore suggests that religion is the indispensable foundation of an intelligent, openhearted approach to life.[46] By relying on beliefs, obligations, and practices, Moore writes that "personal religion is both an awareness of the sacred and a concrete action arising from that awareness."

Religion is meant to be basically about learning to open our hearts, not closing our minds. This is a challenging and profound undertaking. Living a life of goodness, love, and integrity necessitates controlling our impulses and curbing our fears and appetites. It involves dealing with both our weaknesses and our strengths, addressing our moments of fragility, loneliness, and love. It means coping with times when we feel lost and without purpose. To do these things, we must embrace the constant state of flux in our lives. And we have to acknowledge that the process of maturing is often slow. Along the way, we need to transform isolation into connection and let fear be replaced with awe.

Beyond trying hard to do our best to live consciously, how can we address these challenges? To aid us morally and to help us live together well, our religions have laws, commandments, and codes of conduct. In addition, we have designed, implemented, and enforced secular laws to help us stay in a healthy relationship with each other. Without a doubt, both types of laws can be of enormous value. Nonetheless, many of these secular and nonsecular laws are complicated, hard to follow, counterintuitive, and often subject to interpretation. As a natural by-product of both cultural diversity and cultural insularity, one set of laws may or may not feel like they extend to all people. As a result, unfortunately, it can be argued that these laws are easily misused, abused, and manipulated. Additionally, these laws require that our religious leaders and lawmakers take into consideration the hardships, difficulties, and pain of life.

For many reasons, including the above concerns about the laws, many people have suggested that traditional organized religion requires a complete restructuring from its highest level to its lowest. Regardless of our view on this issue, however, Moore suggests that a personal religion can be invaluable. Such a religion necessarily comes out of our hearts and minds and is customized to align with our individual values and sensibilities. Our own religion needs to be felt and experienced, not merely conceptualized. It needs to be meaningful to us and not just emotional. It needs to be our own and not just an ancient tradition.[47]

A different kind of personal religion asks us to shift from being a follower to being a creator. The religion Moore puts forth is not the docile, rehearsed, and constantly reiterated kind. When he says it is our own, he means that it is not someone else's summary of what actions we should take or characteristics we should possess. As Billy Sunday poignantly said, "Going to church doesn't make you a Christian any more than standing in a garage makes you an automobile." Of course, this point applies to any religion and any place of worship. This personal religion, says Moore, is a combination of individual inspiration and tradition that inspires. It is constantly evolving and rejuvenating itself. It addresses the profound truths that shape our lives.[48]

When Thomas Moore speaks about a religion of one's own, he is not talking about a self-centered, haphazardly assembled, ego-driven spiritual concoction. He is suggesting one that is courageous, deeply rooted, informed, and wise, with an awe-inspiring and transcendent dimension. It can be accomplished inside or outside of a traditional religious organization.[49] It means considering various forms of existence. As Gerard Manley Hopkins said, "To lift up the hands in prayer gives God glory, but a man with a dungfork in his hand, and a woman with a slop pail, give him glory too."

At the end of the day, religion is about what we do and how we act. It is not about our intentions. With this in mind, I think of this Zen mondo: Day after day, Ma-tsu sat in meditation until his master finally questioned him about it. Ma-tsu explained that he was hoping to attain Buddhahood. The master picked up a piece of tile and began to rub it with a stone. When Ma-tsu asked him what he was doing, he replied that he was polishing the tile to make it a mirror. "How can you polish a tile into a mirror?" Ma-tsu asked. "How can one become a Buddha by sitting in meditation?" the master shot back.

In this way, do you have a religion that is your own? Describe it. Will you follow convention or follow your heart? What will it take for you to follow your heart?

Creating a Sacred Community

"Know the One. Love the All." Ts'ao-shan Pen-chi

Whether we are following a traditional religion or our own personal one, being in a sacred community can be quite valuable and can contribute to our ability to thrive. Based on my own experiences, feelings, and reading, especially Ron Wolfson's book *The Spirituality of Welcoming—How to Transform Your Congregation into a Sacred Community*[50] and Lawrence Hoffman's *ReThinking Synagogues: A New Vocabulary for Congregational Life*,[51] which is for people of all faiths, the following elements are involved in making a religious community welcoming, respectful, engaging, and meaningful. I think these points might apply to any place of worship—a church, synagogue, temple, mosque, or other religious gathering place—regardless of religion or denomination. I refer to these as "religious centers."

As Wolfson points out, in a sacred community, "relationships are paramount, worship is engaging, and everyone is learning; healing is offered; and personal and institutional transformation is embraced." Each encounter with attendees and guests is viewed as a chance to foster a distinctive, spiritual, reverent sense of community. In a sacred community, people's lives are enriched with meaning, purpose, connectedness, and a relationship with the divine via prayer, education, and acts of goodness, healing, and lovingkindness.[52]

Wolfson explains that the religious center, especially its spiritual and lay leadership, needs to embrace the task of greeting and honoring all who enter its sphere to become a religious center of relationships. In the community, people express their personal welcome upon encountering a stranger. And we must realize that, to some degree, everyone is a stranger. It is essential to take into account that, increasingly today, religious people of all faiths follow their religion by choice in the face of assimilation and competing social norms. Wolfson points out that to become welcoming, several factors require attention, such as anticipating needs, surpassing expectations, making excellent initial impressions, tailoring services, and accurately recalling people's names.[53]

While social capital bonds people, Hoffman reminds us that as we all know, attempting to penetrate a clique is difficult as there are established barriers for outsiders to gain acceptance. A religious center must not be judgmental of people who lack religious learning. Instead, by recognizing the inherent concept of "gifts," we can rethink religious center membership as a sacred agreement with a community that recognizes, nurtures, and guides our talents and interests, where our gifts and passions are recognized, nourished, and directed toward the benefit of others and doing the work of healing the world.[54] A sacred community adheres to the Foundation for Community Encouragement definition "A true community is inclusive, and its greatest enemy is exclusivity. Groups who exclude others because of religious, ethnic, or more subtle differences are not communities."

Many religious centers neglect to form a bond between the individual and the congregation that is so meaningful and valuable that breaking it would be inconceivable. As a result, numerous individuals go through a revolving cycle of joining and leaving the congregation. People leave a religious center when they no longer need the services they signed up for in the first place. Religious centers focused primarily around programs do not inspire a sense of personal commitment.[55]

Wolfson believes that a person needs to connect with five to seven people to maintain involvement. Small groups are essential. People need to talk of "my pastor," "my rabbi," "my priest," "my pujari," or "my imam." The very sacredness of the community hinges on the quality of the relationships that are formed within it. Members take this on themselves and do not rely on paid staff.[56]

Hoffman warns of a congregation where we invest our time, but not our true selves. One sign of this is that we may sit next to someone at services and remain unaware of their name. In this way, relationships remain shallow. By contrast, a sacred community strengthens interconnectedness and counters feelings of alienation or anonymity.[57]

A religious center is not a building, as Hoffman points out. Instead, the collection of sacred relationships constitute the community along with the equally sacred actions that result from them. A religious center is a place where we know the presence of God among us and honor each other as made in God's image. It is where we celebrate each other's sacred stories. It is where we emulate God.[58]

To have worship be engaging, Wolfson believes it is vital to impart practical teaching at religious services that a person can apply to their life. A religious center must be a spiritual center where people find answers to the questions of meaning and purpose. A sacred community will be a place to answer important questions, including:

What meaning has my life had? What difference did and do I make?

What is my purpose here?

Where can I seek God, uncover God's presence, and recognize godliness in others?

Will this community be there for me? Will it be a community I am invested enough in to be there for its members?[59]

The way to engage people in the community is by doing, serving, and caring actively for others and the natural world. These are rarely done by discussing and arguing in committees, as Wolfson observes in his discussion of congregational life. Part of the problem is that our congregations' priorities frequently revolve around programs and activities, rather than principles or values. He suggests that the most critical gauge of a thriving religious center is the number of individuals whose lives are changed for the better. It's not about membership, affiliation, or numbers.[60]

Culture underlies everything a religious center does. As Hoffman explains, religious center culture is dependent on various factors such as size, style, leadership type, and resource management. It is the "feel" one gets just by being there. And once a culture is established, it is extremely difficult to modify. Remember that "like attracts like." Individuals become members because they like the culture prevalent there.[61]

Culture affects how people behave. It is a natural human psychological desire to maintain control, maximize success, minimize losses, and avoid the shame of appearing incompetent. Rather than investing time and energy in learning, we work at controlling, winning, and looking good. Instead, to be engaged in the transformation to a sacred community, Hoffman says people need to build goodwill into the culture, where people are rewarded for taking chances. A healthy culture understands that people take risks because they are not afraid to fail.[62]

At their best, religious centers are places where individuals can experience healing, not solely because such centers are intended for those who are unwell or struggling with feelings of loneliness, dissatisfaction, or purposelessness, but because healing involves achieving a state of wholeness, nurturing a desire to live, and fostering healthy relationships.[63]

Is your religious center a sacred community? In what ways? What would you like to add or change?

7

GRATITUDE

"The hardest arithmetic to master is that which enables us to count our blessings."

Eric Hoffer

We are more than people enslaved to our feelings, circumstances, and genes. As the following selections discuss, gratitude is something that we can choose, strengthen, and grow. It gives us great strength and opens up options in our lives. The great open secret of gratitude is that it does not depend on external circumstances. Gratitude is the kernel that can flower into everything we need to know. Having gratitude is an essential aspect of thriving.

I am deeply grateful for the life I am living. I am aware of so many fabulous things in my life on a daily basis. These involve my wife, my family, my relationships with friends and colleagues, my health, my career, my attitude toward life, where I live, what I do, and the choices I've made. . . . And I am deeply grateful for all the love I have given and received.

Being Grateful Is Beneficial

"Appreciation is a wonderful thing. It makes what is excellent in others belong to us as well." Voltaire

According to Arthur Brooks, acting grateful can actually make us grateful.[64] Gratitude is like a muscle. The more we do with it, the stronger it gets. Some people are just naturally more grateful than others. Some have a heightened genetic tendency to experience relationship satisfaction, perceived partner responsiveness, and positive emotions. Brooke's writes, "For many people, however, gratitude is difficult because life is difficult. Even beyond deprivation and depression, there are many ordinary circumstances in which gratitude doesn't come easily."

Evidence suggests that we can actively choose to practice gratitude—and that doing so raises our happiness. Acting happy, regardless of feelings, coaxes one's brain into processing positive emotions. In one famous 1993 experiment Brooks writes about, researchers asked human subjects to smile forcibly for 20 seconds, notably around the eyes. They found that this action stimulated brain activity associated with positive emotions. This is not just science; it's also common sense: focusing on good things makes you feel better than focusing on bad things. Building the best life does not require focusing only on good things; instead, it requires rebelling against negative impulses and acting right even when we don't feel like it.

In what ways do you practice being grateful? What can you do to increase your feelings of gratitude?

The two words *thank you* possess the potential to bring about a significant change in our physical and mental well-being, athletic abilities, and achievements.[65] Research shows that grateful people are happier and more likely to maintain good friendships. Expressing gratitude alleviates stress, enhances our ability to think clearly in demanding situations, and supports physical healing. It's actually physiologically impossible to experience stress and gratitude simultaneously. When we are grateful, we fill our body and brain with emotions and endorphins that lift and energize us, instead of releasing stress hormones that wear us down. Gratitude and appreciation are also essential for a healthy work environment. In fact, the primary cause of people quitting their jobs is the lack of recognition and appreciation for their efforts. A simple thank-you and a show of appreciation can create a significant impact.

Are you regularly saying thank you? Review the past day or two. Ask yourself: Did I say thank you to my partner? To my loved ones? To coworkers and employees? To people who served or helped me somehow (even if that was their job)?

In addition to building our own happiness, choosing gratitude can also bring out the best in those around us. Try these strategies: Start with internal gratitude and giving thanks privately. Then move to external gratitude, which focuses on public expression through emails or notes to loved ones, friends, and colleagues. And then, finally, be grateful for little, insignificant trifles. Think of the small things you experience—the smell of fall in the air, the fragment of a song that reminds you of when you were a kid. At those moments, give thanks.

We can be grateful for what we have now and not be consumed by desires for things out of our reach. As the Greek Stoic philosopher Epictetus said, "He is a man of sense who does not grieve for what he has not, but rejoices in what he has."

In a world where many people have significant material wealth and much greed, it helps to consider what a life of abundance consists of. As Lynne Twist said, "True abundance does exist; it flows from sufficiency, in an experience of the beauty and wholeness of what is." This is discussed in chapter 4. We can be grateful for having this perspective.

Clarifying Our Situation

"At what point in our lives do we stop blurring? When do we become crisp individuals? What must we do in order to end these fuzzy identities—to clarify just who we really are?" Douglas Coupland

To help us clarify what we are grateful for, we can ask ourselves these questions:

What do I have enough of?

What do I take for granted?

Whom do I know whom I can never repay?

What is the best mistake I've ever made?

How have I changed for the better?

What skill do I most value in myself?

When has nature taken my breath away?

What are your answers to these questions? What are you grateful for?

Consider the following:

If you have food in the refrigerator, clothes on your back, a roof overhead, and a place to sleep, you are richer than the vast majority of people in this world.

If you have money in the bank and in your wallet, spare change in a dish, and your own computer, you are among the world's most wealthy.

If you woke up this morning with more health than illness, you are more blessed than the many who will not even survive this day.

If you have never experienced fear in battle, the loneliness of imprisonment, the agony of torture, or the pangs of starvation, you are ahead of hundreds of millions of people worldwide.

If you can attend a church, synagogue, mosque, or temple without the fear of harassment, arrest, torture, or death, you are envied by and more blessed than billions of people worldwide.

Which of these apply to you?

For a moment, consider your financial condition. How would your life change if you were suddenly transformed into an impoverished person in the developing world?[66]

First, take out the furniture. Leave just a few old blankets, a kitchen table, and one wooden chair. The car went long ago.

Second, throw out the clothes. Each family member may keep their oldest suit or dress and a shirt or blouse. The head of the family has the only pair of shoes.

Third, all kitchen appliances have already gone. Keep a box of matches, some sugar and salt, a handful of onions, and a dish of dried beans. Rescue those moldy potatoes from the garbage; those are tonight's meal.

Fourth, dismantle the bathroom, shut off the running water, and remove the wiring, lights, and everything else that runs on electricity.

Fifth, take away the house and move the family into the tool shed.

Sixth, by now, all the other houses in the neighborhood are gone. Instead, there are shanties—for the fortunate ones.

Seventh, cancel all the newspapers and magazines. Throw out the books. You won't miss them—you are now illiterate. One radio is now left for the whole shantytown.

Eighth, no more postmen, firefighters, or government services. The two-classroom school is miles away, but only about half the children go anyway.

Ninth, no hospital, no doctor. The nearest clinic is now 10 miles away, with a midwife in charge. Get there by bus or bicycle, if you're lucky enough to have one.

Tenth, throw out your bankbooks, stock certificates, pension plans, insurance policies, and social security records. You have a very small cash hoard.

Eleventh, get out and start cultivating your three acres. Try hard to raise enough money in cash crops, because your landlord wants two-thirds and your local moneylender 10 percent.

Twelfth, find some way for your children to bring in a little extra money so that you have something to eat most days. But it won't be enough to keep bodies healthy, so lop off 25 to 30 years of life expectancy.

What material aspects of your life are you grateful for? Take a few minutes and write down your answers.

Now consider your mental and physical health. If you are well—mentally and physically—you have much to be thankful for. Think about all the people who have chronic illnesses or disabilities, or who are suffering as a result of a severe accident. More than 18 percent of the US adult population each year experience some form of mental illness. They endure conditions such as major depression, schizophrenia, bipolar disorder, obsessive-compulsive disorder, and anxiety disorder. That's one in five adults. And only 41 percent of the US adults with a mental health condition received mental health services in the past year.

Take these things into account: Do you sleep well? Do you have proper nutrition? Are you strong? Flexible? Do you have stamina? Are you physically and mentally stable? Do you have access to good doctors, nurses, and hospitals? Do you have adequate health insurance?

For what physical and mental advantages are you grateful?

Making Gratitude a Habit

"The struggle ends when gratitude begins." Neale Donald Walsh

Being grateful can become a matter of habit. Jeremy Adam Smith, the editor of Greater Good Magazine, has described the following six habits of highly grateful people:[67]

1. They take the good things as gifts, not birthrights

The opposite of gratitude is entitlement, the attitude that people owe you something simply because you're special. Preoccupation with the self can cause us to overlook our advantages and those who helped us, feeling there's no reason to be thankful. The antidote to entitlement is to see that we did not bring ourselves into existence and we were created by a higher power, whether that be God or our parents. And recognize that we are never truly self-sufficient. Humans rely on others for many things, including sustenance and medical care. And we all need love, and for that, we need family, partners, friends, and pets.

2. They're grateful to people, not just things.

While being grateful for things like sunlight and trees may be good for us, our gratitude won't make the trees grow or the sun burn brighter. That's not true of people—people will light up when shown gratitude. Saying thanks to our children might make them happier and strengthen our emotional bond. Expressing gratitude to the person who prepares our coffee can improve social connections by increasing our awareness of our interdependence with others. Studies of gratitude in couples show that spouses signal grateful feelings through more caring and attentive behavior. They ask clarifying questions. They respond to trouble with hugs and to good news with smiles.

3. Grateful people are habitually specific.

They don't say, "I love you because you're so wonderfully wonderful." Instead, the really skilled grateful person will say, "I love you for the pancakes you make when you see I'm hungry and the way you massage my feet after work even when you're really tired and how you give me hugs when I'm sad so that I'll feel better." This makes the expression of gratitude feel more genuine. It demonstrates that the person doing the thanking truly paid attention and isn't just going through the motions. The richest expressions of thanks will acknowledge intentions and describe the value of benefits received.

4. Once in a while, they think about death and loss.

According to several studies, contemplating endings really does make us more grateful for the life we currently have. The same applies to envisioning a positive event that never occurred, like a job promotion. This isn't just a hypothetical idea; by giving up something and experiencing life without it, we can understand its true value. Researchers had people eat a piece of chocolate cake and then told some to resist chocolate for a week and others to binge on it. The people who reported the most happiness were those who abstained. Who were least happy? Those who binged.

5. They take the time to smell the roses or whatever gives them pleasure.

Studies indicate that fully experiencing and relishing positive moments makes those moments more memorable in our minds and enhances the psychological benefits they provide. The key is expressing gratitude for the experience. Other research demonstrates that rituals such as shaking a sugar packet increase people's focus on food, and that increased focus makes the food taste better.

6. **They experience life through a grateful lens.**

It's easy to feel grateful for the good things, but it can be difficult to feel grateful when losing a job, a home, good health, or a large portion of one's retirement savings. In such moments, gratitude becomes a critical cognitive process—a way of thinking about the world that can help us turn disaster into a stepping stone. Even if we have been hurt by someone, if we are willing to look, we can find a reason to be thankful for them. Processing a life experience through a grateful lens does not mean denying negativity. Instead, it means realizing your power to transform an obstacle into an opportunity. It means reframing a loss into a potential gain.

Which gratitude habits are you practicing? Which things are you grateful for?

A Blessing of Gratitude[68]

For the blessings lavished upon us in forest and sea, in mountain and meadow, in rain and sun, we are thankful.
For the blessings implanted within us, joy and peace, meditation and laughter, we are grateful.
For the blessings of friendship and love, of family and community.
For the blessings we ask for and those we cannot ask.
For the blessings bestowed upon us openly and those given to us in secret.

For the blessings we recognize and those we fail to recognize.
For the blessings of our traditions and our holy days.
For the blessings of return and forgiveness, of memory, of vision, and
of hope.
For all these blessings which surround us on every side, we give our
thanks and our gratitude.

8

PURPOSE AND MEANING

"The two most important days of your life are the day you are born and the day you discover why."

Mark Twain

Purpose and meaning in life are closely related to our identity, our ability to manage ourselves, and our sense of spirituality—the understanding that something is going on all the time that is greater than ourselves. Developing our purpose is an active engagement, not a passive one. We can't find our purpose like we might find a $20 bill on the street. Instead, it requires being highly engaged through search, pursuit, discovery, and, ultimately, creation of that purpose.

Since my early years, starting as a teenager in high school, I have been interested in the question of life's purpose. I began asking deeper questions about purpose. How does one live a more authentic life that is more closely aligned with one's true purpose? I've concluded that living authentically and intensely is essentially about discovering purpose. It's about trying to answer the ultimate question: Why was I born? Why was I put into this world? For me, this has led to a deeper sense of spirituality, recognizing that I am part of something much more vast, profound, and holy than little preoccupations. For these and many other important reasons, having purpose and meaning in life is a must if we are to thrive.

Why Are Purpose and Meaning Important?

"He who has a why to live can bear almost any how." Friedrich Nietzsche

Many significant benefits come from having purpose and meaning. When we align more fully with our purpose, life becomes more worth living, authentic, and filled with grace. Among other things, having a purpose gives us energy and a degree of vitality. It gives us strength to continue on in the face of difficulties and resistance, or when progress is slow. Having a purpose also helps in decision-making, clarifying what's important and what can be set aside. And if these are not enough, consider that research indicates that knowing our sense of purpose is worth up to seven years of extra life expectancy. Our journey in life can be more than an adventure or just a courageous act. It can be more—a life lived in self-discovery with meaning and purpose.

Without a meaningful purpose, we can get sidetracked and begin to pursue trivial things. When we are unable to comfortably and proudly accept our inherent importance to our family and society, we become susceptible to the false idols of money, power, status, and toys. Dr. Laura Schlessinger addresses these in her book *Ten*

Stupid Things Men Do to Mess Up Their Lives. Career and life development counselor Darryl Petersen[69] commented that these are the primary "motivators" behind many spiritually empty and personally meaningless jobs, especially corporate and professional positions. As a great career coach, he counseled that authentic self-fulfillment can be achieved by creatively designing a true-self-based and cause-driven career. I can personally testify to this!

Without purpose, our lives can be less happy, and there's a definite chance we won't reach our potential. Abraham Maslow[70] believed that without purpose, a person risks evading their own capacities and possibilities. He thought this could lead to being deeply unhappy for the rest of one's life.[71]

Another critically important thing to consider about having purpose is how our lives can impact those of our children. As Carl Jung said, "Nothing has a stronger influence psychologically on their environment and especially their children than the unlived life of the parent."

There are radically different views of the purpose of life. Sigmund Freud believed that life is primarily a quest for pleasure, while Alfred Adler taught that our purpose is a quest for power. I don't adhere to either of these. Rather, I believe that life is a quest for meaning, as Viktor Frankl wrote about in his book *Man's Search for Meaning*.[72] Frankl says that the most significant task for any person is to find meaning in their life. He says there are three possible sources of meaning:

- In work (doing something we determine for ourselves to be significant)
- In love (caring for another person, not necessarily romantic love)

- In courage during difficult times (such as the death of a child or spouse, wartime, or bankruptcy)

Forces beyond our control can take away everything we possess except one thing—our power to choose how we will respond to the situation. We cannot control what happens in our life, but we can control what we feel and do about what happens to us. Frankl also says that suffering in and by itself is meaningless: we give our suffering meaning by how we respond to it. These things embody a life of purpose and meaning.

Do you have a clear purpose? How do you describe it? You have a finite amount of life force and energy; how will you spend it?

For the reasons discussed above, I highly recommend reading *Designing Your Life: Build a Life That Works for You*. This book came from the most popular course at Stanford. Dave Evans and Bill Burnett, the authors, have also created a workbook as well as a book focused on designing your life at work.

Factors Involved in Creating a Meaningful Life

"Practically speaking, a life that is vowed to simplicity, appropriate boldness, good humor, gratitude, unstinting work and play, and lots of walking brings us close to the actual existing world and its wholeness." Gary Snyder

Now let's look at several aspects that can lead to a life of purpose and meaning. At a basic level, we can look at the parts of a person's life to find purpose. These parts include emotional, social, physical and sexual, financial, intellectual, and spiritual. Values and principles can be included in either the spiritual or intellectual category. How we want to spend our time, what we choose to focus on, and what motivates us are central to this process of developing our purpose and a meaningful life. In order to thrive, we need to sort these things out.

Developing a meaningful life involves many options as to what we focus on. Our focus can reflect choices ranging from more to less meaningful and from things we might consider glamorous to simple things. The more meaning we find in life, the happier we typically feel, and the more often we feel encouraged to pursue even greater meaning and purpose. According to research cited by Jill Suttie and Jason Marsh in their Greater Good article "Is a Happy Life Different from a Meaningful One?" meaningfulness compares and contrasts with happiness in these ways:

- Thinking about the past, present, and future—and the relationship between them—is linked to meaningfulness. Happiness revolves around a focus on the present.
- Health, wealth, and ease in life are all related to happiness, but not meaning.
- Social connections are linked to both meaningfulness and happiness. Meaningfulness is related to what one gives to others; for example, taking care of children. Happiness comes largely from the benefits one receives from social relationships, especially friendships.
- Engaging in challenging or difficult situations that are beyond oneself or one's pleasure promotes meaningfulness, but not happiness.
- Doing things to express oneself and caring about personal and cultural identity are related to a meaningful life, but not a happy one.[73]

It might be helpful and valuable to create a balance between meaningful pursuits and happiness in our lives as we grow, nurture relationships with family and friends, and engage in the world.

What are you doing that creates a sense of meaning and purpose? What would you like to do more of?

Additionally, we have choices about how to focus our time and attention. We can focus and work on things that are urgent or nonurgent and on things that are important or unimportant. We can use our time effectively, not just efficiently. The diagram below shows these as four quadrants:[74]

	Urgent	Not Urgent
Important	Quadrant 1 **Do**	Quadrant 2 **Schedule**
Not Important	Quadrant 3 **Delegate**	Quadrant 4 **Delete**

Quadrant 1, **Urgent and Important**, involves activities that have outcomes that lead to achieving our goals, whether these are professional or personal. Urgent activities demand immediate attention and may involve a crisis. They are often associated with achieving someone else's goals. Examples might be an emergency surgery, a term paper, or a tax deadline. We have to do these things *now*.

Quadrant 2, **Not Urgent but Important**, allows us to take the time to think longer term and more strategically. Here we can focus on goals and planning. An example is a CEO of a well-run company with an executive team handling day-to-day operations. Another example is research into things like a cure for cancer. Schedule time to do this work.

Quadrant 3, **Urgent but Not Important**, encompasses situations in which there are many ongoing demands on us but the importance of these demands is low. Urgent but unimportant activities are things that sap our time and energy without contributing to longer-term benefits. They keep us busy but have no real value. Unexpected texts or phone calls are examples. It's best to delegate or reschedule these as much as possible.

Quadrant 4, **Not Urgent and Not Important**, involves distractions. Life can be full of these. Examples include posting on Facebook, engaging in gossip with coworkers, and reading unproductive email threads. Eliminate these as often as possible.

Where is your focus? Where do you want it to be?

It is helpful to realize that our lives can be focused on different arenas of life. We can think of this as three different economies. One is the market economy, which includes the business world, where services are offered and products are produced. The output of the market economy has a lot to do with earning **money**. A second economy is the social economy, which includes the nonprofit world, government, and foundations and is fundamentally about helping others and our planet. Teaching and health care can be included in this economy. The outcome of the social economy revolves around having an **impact**. The third economy is the creative economy, which includes performing and visual arts. The creative economy's output is **expression**, including creating works of art in various forms. As these three economies have significantly different outcomes, it might be helpful to understand which one you are most aligned with. Sometimes we can combine these to create a more balanced, productive, healthy, and happy life.

Which economy is most important to you? How important to you is making money versus having an impact versus being creative?

If you could choose anything, what work would you do, and how would you spend your time? To help with this, consider these questions: Is it using your skills and talents? Does it fit your values? Does it have the right amount of challenge? Is it fun? Are you learning? Does it keep you physically and mentally sharp? Is it keeping you current and plugged in? Does it have the right amount of solo versus group time? Do you have time to recharge?

In a directly related way, when thinking about engaging in a new project, maybe when considering a new job, recruiting a new employee, or embarking as a start-up entrepreneur, keep in mind the three necessary conditions for meaningful work:

1. It needs to be sufficiently complex.
2. It needs to have enough autonomy.
3. There needs to be a clear relationship between effort and reward.

And it might be helpful to ask these questions to see if it is meaningful: Is it significant? Is it ethical? Can it be measurably effective? Is it transformative? Is it novel? Will it be enduring? Sometimes it may not be realistic to factor all of these into our decision, but they are worth considering and could result in something better than we realize.

In what ways is your work meaningful? Which conditions exist or are absent?

Clarifying the issues above can help us enormously to position ourselves with what we consider to be meaningful work and in our lives in general. It might not be possible to create something that fits everything we are looking for—the goal is not about perfection as much as it is about finding or creating a decisively strong fit with our values, talents, skills, and things that we want to put our life energy into.

Writing a Vision Statement and Living a Legacy

"If my mind can conceive it, and my heart can believe it— then I can achieve it." Muhammad Ali

Writing a vision statement can be of great value in creating your purpose. It can have great power too. Your vision statement might include sections outlining your core values and beliefs, your unique talents and gifts, your purpose, and your mission over the next long period, such as 10 years. Having written my own vision statement, I've found that reviewing it and revising it periodically has been immensely helpful in my life. It has clarified things and empowered me to act. I urge you to write your own.

Here are my core values and beliefs, as well as my revised statement of purpose:

My Core Values and Beliefs

- I intend to contribute to making both the natural and the human world a better place.
- I believe we can and must design for ecological sustainability and for a world that works for everyone.
- I believe that we must employ whole-systems thinking and collaboration to deal with the challenges and complexities of our world.
- I believe that economic sustainability, while not a sole goal in our lives, must result from our work.
- I believe that the heart of implementation and long-term success is through the creation of relationships and community.
- I am dedicated to quality—quality of service, quality of relationships, quality of communication, and quality of promises.
- I am committed to providing an opportunity to realize the potential for all I am involved with. I believe that everyone can contribute in their own way.
- I am committed to the highest standards of ethics and integrity.

My Life Purpose

My purpose is to be a role model by honoring my values and beliefs and using my unique gifts to create solutions that protect the environment and improve the quality of life. Specifically, my purpose is fivefold:

1. To make the world a better place.
2. To be supportive, caring, empathetic, and compassionate with my family and friends. To be a positive role model, being kind, generous, thoughtful, loving, appreciative, trustworthy,

humorous, a good listener, humble, patient, and strong like a willow branch rather than a piece of oak.

3. To use my financial wealth to be philanthropic, focusing on the sources of problems rather than on symptoms.

4. To be a lifelong learner, which encourages me to read, travel, have new experiences, meet interesting and stimulating people, take appropriate risks, experiment, and try new things. Most importantly, to continue to evolve and gain wisdom.

5. To die as old as possible and as fit as possible, which requires that I take care of myself physically, mentally, emotionally, and spiritually. To live with vitality, recognizing that life is about intensity, not longevity.

Have you written a vision statement? If so, when did you last review and revise it? If not yet, when will you?

Of course, in developing a purpose and vision statement, there are many possibilities to consider. One approach that helps is to review the world's most critical problems today, or maybe those in your local community. **As you think about each one, is there one you especially care about? What role could you play in improving the situation? What thoughts do you have about how we can effectively address the problem? What will it realistically take to have a meaningful impact?**

There are a number of specific issues that concern me. For example, it can be argued that one of the roots of our problems is a loss of vision and a loss of hope, which have been replaced by deep resignation. People are resigned to not making a difference. What can be done about this? How can a greater sense of personal and organizational vision be developed and cultivated?

How can we engage more in dialogue with each other rather than engage in debate or not listen at all to a different view?

Social change is quite complex. Often it occurs very slowly, and often efforts seem just an experiment. What can we do to cause the change we want and need to happen faster and be more likely to succeed?

What issues are most important to you?

In addition to writing a vision statement, we can significantly impact and reinforce our purpose by clarifying our legacy now, while we are alive and vital. As Thomas Moore said, "Legacy is a way to age well—a source of joy and a feeling of fulfillment." Legacy is often thought to be the cumulative aspect of the life we have lived, to be written on a tombstone—this is capital-*L* Legacy. This capital-*L* Legacy can be one through which we pass on our wisdom and leave something of value for future generations.

Legacy is also, and maybe even more importantly, about the little-*l* legacy. This type of legacy could be a role we played for only a brief period, perhaps in a job or a relationship. It can also reflect how we are living life now, today. This is also discussed as part of evolving in chapter 13.

In my own life, with everything I do and in each relationship, I am trying to continue to live and build on the following four legacy components:

Excellence   **Purpose**   **Encouragement**   **Love**

What legacy do you want to build during your lifetime and then leave behind?

During the expanse of a lifetime, as significant things in our lives change, it might be valuable to reinvent ourselves, to allow new things to emerge, and to change our definition of our life purpose. You'll find more about this also in chapter 13.

Have you changed your life purpose as your life has changed? If so, in what specific ways?

I want to end this chapter with the following prayer:

Make us ever mindful of thy presence.

Inspire us with our life's purpose,

That we may use our time on earth, however brief,

To transform not only ourselves

But our planet into a place

Of vision and compassion,

Creativity and peace.

SECTION II

THRIVING TOGETHER

"Coming together is a beginning;

keeping together is progress;

working together is success."

Henry Ford

Thriving Together

9 - Relationships with Others

- Types of Relationships
- Building Relationships
- Communicating
- Relationships in the Family
- Building Relationships in a Community

10 - Leadership and Management

- Roles, Traits, Qualities, and Styles
- Reciprocal Relationships
- Habits for Success and Best Practices

9

RELATIONSHIPS WITH OTHERS

"Treasure your relationships, not your possessions."

Anthony J. D'Angelo

What would our life be without relationships with others? There are a wide variety of relationships and many types. Some are casual; others are intimate. They are in every part of our lives—at work, in play, with family, and in spiritual and religious matters. The quality of our relationships with others reflects the quality of our relationship with ourselves, as discussed in chapter 2. Relationships are also vital to avoiding conflicts and war because, as we continue to see, we become more tribal as we become more global. Overall, there are many things about forming, strengthening, and keeping relationships with others that can be learned, and actions that can be avoided. We have the power to build and deepen our relationships and thereby thrive.

I am very fortunate to have had important relationships and friendships throughout my life. These are relationships in which we took the time to get to know each other, cared about each other, and "invested" in each other. Relationships and friendships take a lot of work, and I regularly spend time trying to understand them and improve them. Relationships with others have been the source of the biggest joys and the most significant challenges I have faced in life, as they can result in powerful emotions ranging from deep caring and love to anger and pain. I am also aware that I have made mistakes, caused pain, and been arrogant and insensitive along the way. I have had to grow and change.

Types of Relationships

"The glory of friendship is not the outstretched hand nor the kindly smile, nor the joy of companionship; it is the spiritual inspiration that comes to one when he discovers that someone else believes in him and is willing to trust him." Ralph Waldo Emerson

In reviewing relationships, it has been suggested that there are three levels of relationships: pleasant, engaging, and meaningful. Pleasant relationships are those that are easygoing and enjoyable. Engaging relationships typically are established among colleagues who share a similar wavelength. Meaningful relationships, however, arise when people sense that they are serving a purpose greater than themselves. A meaningful relationship elevates the parties to a higher plane. It connects people with a higher purpose, a cause. Creating and sustaining meaningful relationships takes work. They can link us to another person in a way that is comfortable, sometimes challenging, and often fulfilling.

Take a look at your relationships. Which are in the "pleasant" category? Which are engaging? Which are meaningful?

The type and depth of our relationship with another person can also relate to the outcomes experienced. This point is reflected in the chart below:

	Low Outcomes	High Outcomes
Relationships High	Accommodate	Collaborate
Relationships Low	Avoid	Compete

Take a look at your relationships. Where do they fall in this framework? Where do you thrive? How many relationships do you have in which you can collaborate?

Another relationship framework, according to Nathan Hill in his book *The Nix*, is one in which we see people in our lives as either enemies, obstacles, traps, or puzzles. If we see people as enemies, obstacles, or traps, we will constantly be in conflict with them and ourselves. Alternatively, if we see people as puzzles, and we see ourselves as a puzzle, then we will always be intrigued, and we will discover commonalities with another person.[75] In addition to looking at people as puzzles, we can recognize that humor shapes relationships. We make a choice about whom to associate with based on humor alone. Remember that we have the power to reframe and change the way we view others.

How do you see people? When do you see yourself and others as puzzles? Who is in your humor tribe?

Friendship is considered one of the rarest and most demanding but also most rewarding kinds of human relationships. There are three kinds of friendships: those founded on mutual utility, those based on pleasure, and those founded on virtue. Many people make friends early in life, before they are 25 or so. It is much harder to make friends later in life, but it is nonetheless very valuable and worthwhile. Having friends of all ages leads to health and vitality, allowing us to learn and share our experiences and wisdom. In a true friendship, we never need to hide who we really are. Being who we really are is what makes relationships work. Friendship and deep relationship are about being authentic and genuine, which is very appealing and is another aspect of thriving.

I especially like this piece from an unknown author on friendship:

It's as old as man himself, yet as new as this moment or the next. It's ever-changing, and sometimes it is ever-constant. It's stronger than any wall ever built. It overcomes politics and national barriers. It can't be blinded by strange customs or blocked by foreign languages. It has been written about and analyzed by wise men, yet it has never been defined, and never will be.

You can't see it, yet it is everywhere. It survives weakness and neglect and thrives on thoughtfulness. Its possibilities are infinite, its strength limitless. It's what makes a man human, what makes life worth living. It's friendship.

In considering these aspects, which of your relationships are true friendships? Review each one. What is the friendship based on?

An important relationship choice is whether we are loyal to family and friends. This involves many things, including having strong feelings, staying steadfast in your support and allegiance, keeping your word, following through on your commitments, proving you can be relied on, keeping promises and the other person's secrets, and not keeping secrets from the other person.

Are you loyal? Give examples. When were you not loyal? Why?

One of the most important relationships we can have in our lives is with a partner, which often leads to marriage. Unfortunately, the percentage of people getting divorced is quite high. A few years ago, the *New York Times* published a list of 13 questions to ask before getting married. The questions can be reviewed here:

https://www.nytimes.com/interactive/2016/03/23/fashion/weddings/marriage-questions.html?searchResultPosition=1

I highly recommend asking these questions before you marry (or, better yet, before you get engaged). You might also suggest to someone you love or care about who is considering getting married that they check this out. These questions can also be valuable to discuss long after you are married!

I want to end this section about types of relationships with the question: What makes a relationship healthy? Consider this piece originally written by Howard Hunter:

Mend a quarrel. Seek out a forgotten friend. Dismiss suspicion and replace it with trust. Write a letter. Share some treasure. Give a soft answer. Encourage youth. Manifest your loyalty in word and deed.

Keep a promise. Forgo a grudge. Forgive an enemy. Apologize. Try to understand. Examine your demands on others. Think first of someone else. Be kind. Be gentle. Laugh a little more.

Express your gratitude. Welcome a stranger. Gladden the heart of a child. Take pleasure in the beauty and wonder of the earth. Speak your love and then speak it once again.[76]

Review your relationships. Which are healthy? What can you do to make your relationships better?

Building Relationships

"The deepest principle in human nature is the craving to be appreciated." William James

There are many aspects to building a relationship. People are complex, and so are their needs and expectations. It's much easier, maybe even essential, in building relationships and forming friendships to be easy to be around, to be pleasant, or even fun. Be agreeable, not disagreeable. Building a close relationship often requires that trust is established, and to maintain the trust, communication needs to be open and honest. There are also many ways in which a relationship can be held back or damaged. These are discussed below.

It's important to appreciate that building harmonious relationships is hard to do and takes a certain amount of maturity and wisdom. According to Thomas Moore,[77] the reasons why it's hard to have a harmonious relationship include the following:

First of all, humans are often motivated by emotions—sometimes unsettled ones—rather than by reason or logic. We often have no idea why we do and say the things we do. We can experience sudden impulses, such as love, anger, fear, or aggression and violence, that can overpower us without warning.

Second, we're all complex and multifaceted beings with many layers of depth. As a result, we can never fully know ourselves or our own motives.

Third, a significant portion of our actions and reactions are based on past experiences, particularly from very early childhood. They stay with us, and they continue to play out as important themes in our identity. And we are often unaware of this until they are brought to our attention.

Fourth, many past negative patterns persist and continue to shape our thoughts and actions without much change. The good news is that these are not unchangeable; among other things, if the issues are very serious, counseling can help.

According to relationship expert John Gottman, there is a ladder of needs within relationships, especially friendships. He writes in *The Relationship Cure: A 5 Step Guide to Strengthening Your Marriage, Family, and Friendships*[78] that building relationships involves making and responding to bids, which include questions, statements, and comments. Nonverbal bids include facial expressions, affiliating gestures (such as opening the door, offering a place to sit, handing a utensil), vocalizing (including laughing, grunting, sighing, and groaning), and playful or affectionate touching. In responding to a bid, you can turn toward, turn away, or turn against the other person. Here's Gottman's ladder of friendship needs:

1. Light conversation
2. Humor
3. Friendly gossip
4. Affection
5. Support
6. Problem-solving
7. Connection around heartfelt subjects (goals, worries, values, meaning)

Take a look at each of your friendships and close relationships. Where are they on this ladder? What will it take for you to go to a higher rung?

In this same vein, a few years ago I wrote a short piece called "Ten Steps in Building Relationships and Friendships." These steps, from lowest to highest, are:

Walk by without seeing or acknowledging . . .

Ignore; next, Nod, have slight eye contact . . .

Acknowledge (cold); next, Nod, smile, say hello . . .

Acknowledge (warm); next, Shake hands, greet, or air kiss . . .

Greet; next, Stop, brief chat . . .

Friendly (casual); next, Longer chat . . .

Friendly (deeper); then Long chat, about personal facts, circumstances . . .

Relating (mind); then Plan something together for the future . . .

Liking and Friendship; then Longer chat about feelings . . .

Relating (heart); the highest step is to Check in with mind

and heart, share personal feelings and experiences, listen and ask questions, show affection, and be vulnerable . . .

Caring relationship

Take a look at each of your relationships and your relationships overall. Where are they in terms of these steps above?

Esther Wojcicki writes about the fundamental ingredients of relationships in her book *How to Raise Successful People: Simple Lessons for Radical Results.*[79] She uses the acronym **TRICK** to sum them up:

T—Trust

R—Respect

I—Independence

C—Collaboration

K—Kindness

Review each of your key relationships. Where are they in terms of TRICK?

As Carolyn Shaffer and Kristin Anundsen write in *Creating Community Anywhere*, becoming successful and developing successful relationships with others starts with having a sincere interest in others. We also need to develop certain qualities.[80] These include:

Openness and flexibility. This means not only tolerating diversity and different opinions but also welcoming them. Successful relationships recognize and appreciate that other people have different ways of viewing and approaching things. If others tell us only what we want to hear, we miss the true richness of relationships and community. As Mary Engelbreit wrote, "Flexible people never get bent out of shape."

Willingness to abide by community or group agreements. For some people, this can be difficult, as they view interdependence as a threat. When they realize their identity is not defined by any group, they can relax and uphold agreements, knowing their inner integrity will not be threatened. They can move from "I" to "we" without losing "I." But along the way, it's vital not to surrender our sense of values and ethics. It's better to walk alone than with others going in the wrong direction.

Willingness to pursue group goals. This may entail placing group goals ahead of certain individual ones at times. It requires trusting that eventually individual needs will be served.

Willingness to risk asserting ourselves. Taking the initiative and disagreeing when necessary are as essential to healthy relationships as is the willingness to get along with others. To become closer, it may be necessary to risk some painful interactions. But remember what Eleanor Roosevelt said: "No one can make you feel inferior without your consent."

Willingness to practice the skills that enhance relationships. These include communication skills—listening well, asking questions, and speaking with clarity—as well as conflict resolution and decision-making skills.

Desire to see ourselves as we really are and others as they really are. It's important to accept who we are, both the good and the parts we'd like to improve. Accept that there are things you can't change—for example, how tall you are, how smart you are, or your race. And realize that there are things that you can change with work. The same goes for how you see others.

Willingness to give and receive. This includes being willing to take care of others and have them take care of us.

A commitment to see it through. This means we must keep at it despite conflict, changing individual needs, other demands on our time, and the shared pains of implementation.

Which of these qualities do you have? Which ones require more effort on your part?

Within a relationship and the many interactions and events involved, it's very valuable to be clear about what our and the other person's expectations are. In many cases, it helps actually to discuss these. During such a discussion, it's best to listen. Remember that this is not a debate. Expectations often have important emotions embedded in them.

Relationships are like a bank where we make deposits and withdrawals. We need to watch closely, be sensitive, and understand what positive things we do that lead to a deposit and which negative things lead to a withdrawal. Depending on the person we have a relationship with, it might take five deposits to offset one withdrawal. In other relationships, that ratio might be higher, even much higher—like perhaps 20 deposits to offset one withdrawal. To build a relationship, make as many deposits as possible and resist making withdrawals!

One defining quality in a deep friendship, and really every important relationship, is the ability to give and receive feedback. Deep relationships are based on trust and allow for candid feedback, whether asked for or unsolicited. My experience is that there's precious little honest, constructive feedback in most relationships.

Giving feedback involves taking a risk and being committed to the other person. Be clear about why you are giving the feedback. Is it for pure and good reasons—to help the other person? Or is it to show that you know better and have more power in the relationship? We must be kind, listen well, and pick our time to provide feedback. When embarking on the conversation, ask them if this is a good time to discuss the issue. If the other person is not ready or receptive, it might be best overall—for the other person and for the relationship— to forgo the conversation (at least for now).

Are you giving and receiving constructive feedback? With whom? About what? How's it working out?

Being willing to be vulnerable can also expand a relationship. About 15 years ago, I felt my life was going well. So, I asked myself, "What could make my life even better?" After mulling this over, the answer was clear—while I had a number of friends, I wanted to deepen those relationships if possible. I wondered how this could happen. And I realized that I needed to be more open and vulnerable in those relationships. I decided to take the risk with four long-term friends, knowing that there was the possibility that nothing would change and that I would have to be prepared for that outcome. After I began being more open and vulnerable, to my absolute delight, three of these friends started opening up more to me, sharing concerns, doubts, and stories about themselves that I never knew. Our friendships deepened. This was an enormous gift to each of them and to me.

In what ways are you letting yourself be vulnerable in your relationships with others?

We regularly face challenges in our relationships with others. This also ushers in choice. In handling a problem we are having with another person, we have options:

We can fight, be angry, attack, criticize, be miserable, and make others miserable, OR

We can resist or avoid, keep our distance, ignore, discourage unwelcome behavior, withhold attention, not laugh at the other person's attempts at humor, OR

We can accept, take the high road, be empathetic, be optimistic about the progress made in building the relationship, OR

We can embrace the relationship as it is, enjoy the good qualities in the other person, find things to like in them, look forward to seeing and speaking with them, and lean in.

What difficult relationship choices are you making? Take your time as you consider this.

There are times when, in order to keep a relationship healthy, we need to apologize, especially to friends and loved ones. Sometimes apologizing is important because it's doing the right thing if we make a mistake or hurt them, intentionally or not—but it is also a very important, maybe essential, way to keep the relationship healthy. As Kevin Hancock explained, "Apologies aren't meant to change the past; they are meant to change the future." When we make a mistake and hurt someone, we can own up to it. We can apologize and work hard to fix it. See the section on forgiveness in chapter 5.

Additionally, consider the ways in which you can expand or limit the depth of your relationships. Are you letting yourself feel and express your feelings, or are you holding back? Is the relationship more about thinking? How judgmental are you? A strong relationship will have enough safety, trust, and room to allow you to be honest and confront issues without withholding or just walking away.

We often undermine our relationships with others, and we damage ourselves, as discussed in chapter 2. This is due to habits of the mind. Shirzad Chamine's book *Positive Intelligence*[81] does a great job of explaining and deciphering these harmful habits of the mind. Much of this can be avoided. The good news is that we have a sage self that can come to our rescue and help keep a relationship healthy and intact. This book was highly beneficial to me. I encourage you to read it!

I have found that maintaining relationships requires dedication and commitment. In today's world, people live complex, demanding lives. Maintaining a friendship is extra hard if we don't live near our friends and rarely have an opportunity to be together. I decided to commit to staying in touch with friends, knowing how important this aspect is to my life (and I hope to theirs). I do this even if it seems that I am usually the one initiating contact. I am okay with this, as long as I see that the friend is excited to hear from me and appreciates our relationship.

It's also important to realize that sometimes a relationship reaches its natural end. That's okay too. People move on and grow apart. Try your best to leave on good terms. As some wise soul said, "Never miss an opportunity to make others happy, even if you have to leave them in order to do it."

Communicating

"Any problem, big or small, within a family always seems to start with bad communication. Someone isn't listening." Emma Thompson

The quality of our relationships is closely tied to how we communicate. It's enormously important that we listen. Listening is about being present, not just being quiet. And when we talk, often what we say leads to uncomfortableness with others. It will help to get into the habit of saying "Yes, *and* . . ." rather than "Yes, *but* . . ." or even "No." And in relationships and communication with others overall, don't fight fire with fire. It only serves to heat things up.

Before we speak, it's wise to **THINK** about the following questions:

T—Is it **T**rue?

H—Is it **H**elpful?

I—Is it **I**nspiring?

N—Is it **N**ecessary?

K—Is it **K**ind?

Recall the past few days and the things you've said. Give examples of when you spoke with every part of THINK. Recall when you missed one or more of these elements. Which one(s)? Is there a pattern?

Practicing the skill of Intentional Dialogue can be a helpful approach to building or rebuilding a difficult relationship. It often takes a lot of practice and may even require the assistance of a trained facilitator. Several years ago, my daughter and I went to a facilitator, a licensed clinical social worker, to work out some of the issues between us. In these sessions, we learned to use the Intentional Dialogue approach. It certainly was not our natural way of communicating (or, more honestly, how we were miscommunicating). These sessions were enormously helpful, and our relationship improved markedly. Heartfelt thanks, Barbara!

Intentional Dialogue creates connection and meaningful contact. It increases the chance that we will feel heard, understood, and seen. It creates safety. It involves generous listening, not judging, and not interpreting. Intentional Dialogue includes:

Mirroring—"What I'm hearing you say is . . ." "Did I get that right?" "Is there more about that?"

Summarizing—"So, let me see if I've gotten it all. . . ."

Validating—"I understand what you're saying, and it makes sense to me because . . ." If it doesn't make sense, say, "Help me understand."

Empathizing. "I can imagine how you feel. . . ." Ask, "Is there more about that?"

One communication trap is to debate rather than to enter into a dialogue with another person with whom we have, or want to have, a relationship. Learning to dialogue is so critically important in the world today that Condoleezza Rice, former US Secretary of State,[82] made a point of this. When she was asked recently at a Stanford Alumni event what is the most critical challenge facing Stanford University today, she answered immediately that it was for the students to learn to listen to each other, especially when they didn't agree, and begin to dialogue.

In his book *The Magic of Dialogue: Transforming Conflict into Cooperation*, Daniel Yankelovich explains the difference between dialogue and debate. Dialogue is about learning. Debate is about winning. Dialogue assumes that others have a piece of the answer. It's collaborative, looking for shared understanding and finding common ground. This requires us to listen in order to learn, understand, and find a basis for agreement. And when we speak, it's best to share our own experiences. Debate assumes there is only one correct answer, and we have it. It's combative, attempting to prove the other side wrong. It's about winning, listening to find flaws, and making counterarguments.[83]

The difference between debate and dialogue is roughly summarized below:

Debate	Dialogue
* Assumes there is a correct answer, and I have it	* Assumes that many people have pieces of the answer and together they can craft a solution
* Is combative; participants attempt to prove the other side wrong	* Is collaborative; participants work together toward a common understanding
* Is about winning	* Is about exploring the common good
* Entails listening to find flaws and make counter-arguments	* Entails listening to understand and find meaning and agreement
* Is about seeking a conclusion or vote that ratifies my position	* Is about discovering new options

How do you assess your relationship communications? Consider these questions: Are you saying, "Yes, and . . . "? Are you in dialogue or debate? Are you listening to understand? Give examples. What could you do better?

Relationships in the Family

"Rules without relationship lead to rebellion." Josh McDowell

Relationships within families can be incredibly complex. If you are like me, you find relationships with friends to be easier than those with family members, in large part because relationships with friends are voluntary. Even as adults, we are often impacted by our parents, even long after they are no longer alive. And as a result, our relationship with ourselves can be dramatically affected, as discussed in chapter 2. As we become fully mature, we can better understand our relationships with our parents and ourselves.

I see that I had a superb mother who gave me unconditional love. A number of my fundamental values came from her—my love of animals, my interest in science and history, and the pleasure and importance of reading. Mom taught me how to play bridge and Scrabble and tennis. My relationship with her has always been easy, even during these last 10 years, when I have been her primary caregiver.

My father is an entirely different story. He is a guiding light, mentor, and teacher to me. I respect him. He is remarkable in many ways, including being a highly decorated veteran. Among the over two dozen military medals he was awarded, he earned the Bronze Star twice and the Purple Heart. On top of these medals, a few years ago he was knighted by France and became a Chevalier of the Legion of Honor. I learned a lot from him, including how to be logical and disciplined. He is strong, a man of principle, and has made a difference in many people's lives. Yet as much as I respect him and owe him so much for my good qualities, our relationship has been challenging for much of my life.

How is your relationship with your mother? Your father? Your children, if you have any?

Because of this complex relationship with my father, I have spent a lot of time over the years trying to sort things out and reading about fathers. I found Samuel Osherson's book *Finding Our Fathers: The Unfinished Business of Manhood*[84] particularly helpful. Many sons don't have an opportunity to know their fathers, often because child-rearing is so tied to mothers in our society. Fathers are often mysterious to their sons because fathers' identities are locked up in work. What seems to characterize the father-son relationship is difficulty bridging the gap between them. Fathers and sons often only speak the language of action-related activities such as sports, but not usually the language of caring. The language of caring is not one that fathers and sons typically develop. It's one they have to learn when they're both adults.

It's not uncommon for fathers to die before relationships are worked out, as Osherson explains. Some men continue to work on the relationship after death. The relationship can still be healed then, although it's more difficult because we no longer have direct contact. But the task is the same—transforming that inner memory we carry around of our fathers from critical and judgmental to caring and nurturing. As Anne Sexton said, "It doesn't matter who my father was; it only matters who I remember he was."

How does this healing happen when the father has died? Sons report writing letters to their dead fathers, letters which obviously are not mailed. They say what they wish they had said to their fathers and imagine their fathers responding. Some men can find the journals or diaries of their fathers to learn more about them. Or they can talk to relatives or acquaintances to learn more about sides of their fathers they never knew. Even imaginary dialogues can be helpful. What is essential is to find the thread of caring that leaves us feeling respected and good about ourselves.[85]

In my case, I wrote two letters to my father but did not send them. On the advice of a psychologist friend, I wrote the letters to the father I wished I had and felt I deserved. One letter focused on the strength of our relationship, our love and respect for each other, and our open and caring communication. The second letter described an imaginary weekend we had spent together, filled with happiness and fun activities together. Writing these two letters was very cathartic for me. I was able, in essence, to create a second father who had the relationship with me that I yearned for. These unsent letters allowed me to let go of most of the pain and disappointment I had felt with my real father.

Do you feel good or bad, respected and loved or not, when you consider your father (or mother)? Give examples. Consider speaking with him (or her) or writing a letter, even if you don't send it.

Considering family relationships, I'd like to offer a few comments on parenting. Parents often say that their kids are growing up too fast. While I certainly understand what they are saying, it is possible to slow things down. With focus and commitment, it is possible to stay close to our children, to ask open questions, to know who their friends are, to invite their friends over, to go to their school, sporting, and cultural events together, and overall to be a part of their daily lives. It's important to celebrate each step along the way and to keep our eyes open. We can model how healthy relationships work. For example, ask your children about their relationships first, not their grades. All of this is critically important if one or both parents have demanding careers, if they have to travel often, or if there is only one parent in the household.

Many parents think their job is to make sure their child avoids falling into one of life's inevitable "potholes." Frankly, I don't believe this is the job of a caring, committed parent. Instead, I think the parent's job is to provide the child with the mental and emotional tools to get out of the pothole by themselves. At the same time, the parent needs to make sure the child knows their parent cares and that if they need help from the parent, the parent will always reach out a hand to help them get back on their feet. It's important to remember that some of the most important things to learn in life come from mistakes, especially those that have caused us and others pain. It's vital to learn to take responsibility. This applies not only to ourselves but also to our children. We can wisely avoid robbing our children of these opportunities to try new things, take responsibility, take a risk, and even sometimes fail.

Another aspect of being a healthy parent is watching closely and "adjusting the bar." What I mean by this is that our child may sometimes find something too easy. Think of a level of reading or math. If the learning is too easy, raising the bar is appropriate. Sometimes the school can help with this, and at other times, the parent needs to find resources outside the school program. The same logic goes for those times when a child is struggling. If something is too hard, it can erode the child's self-esteem and maybe even open them up to ridicule from others. Again, some intervention by the parent may be called for. This might mean adjusting the bar so that the child can be successful.

One of parents' hardest and most challenging jobs is deciding whether and how to intervene—in things like changing schools, helping the child replace friends, and "adjusting the bar" as described above. Significant interventions are extra challenging if the two parents don't agree on the best solution to try. This is where listening comes in! We're best off if we don't make it a debate.

As our children grow and mature, our role in their lives necessarily changes. And, especially in their teenage years, they might want and need more distance. At this time, it might help to realize that our task is ultimately to have them successfully launch and be healthy and independent, able to stand solidly on their own two feet.

In what ways are you a good parent? In which ways can you be even better? Do you recognize and are you addressing any unhealthy family patterns?

Two final notes on family relationships: First, family traditions are worth honing. They are the glue to family and help create meaning over time. In my family, we have developed a number of family traditions, one of which is giving family or group hugs. We also have a tradition of asking everyone to comment on Friday night about the highlights of their week. I know a family that asks each other to say one thing they appreciate about the person after they blow out the candles on their birthday cake. And my second note: if we have a small or not particularly close family, we can invite people into our families, such as an honorary uncle, aunt, or some other title. For our family, this has been a very rich addition.

To Love and to Care—A Family Prayer

We thank You, O God, for our family and what we mean and bring to one another. We are grateful for the bonds of loyalty and affection that sustain us, and that keep us close to one another no matter how far apart we may be.

We thank you for implanting within us a deep need for each other and for giving us the capacity to love and to care.

Help us to be modest in our demands of one another but generous in our giving to each other. May we never measure how much love or encouragement we offer; may we never count the times we forgive. Instead, may we always be grateful that we have one another and that we are able to express our love in acts of kindness.

Keep us gentle in our speech. When we offer words of criticism, may they be chosen with care and spoken softly. May we waste no opportunity to speak words of sympathy, appreciation, or praise.

Bless our family with health, happiness, and contentment. Above all, grant us the wisdom to build a joyous and peaceful home in which Your spirit will always abide.

Building Relationships in a Community

"And remember, we all stumble, every one of us. That's why it's a comfort to go hand in hand." Emily Kimbrough

As we go through life, and especially as we age, there is a need to be in a community. A group becomes a community in somewhat the same way that a stone becomes a gem—through a process of cutting and polishing. The vast majority of people can learn the rules of communication and community building and are willing to follow them. The following, written by Robert Gilman, are guidelines for the process of creating a closer community:

Recognize it will be a journey and enjoy it.

Establishing a community takes a significant amount of time, often spanning several years. The Dalai Lama said three conditions make it possible to create a community: great love, great persistence, and great patience. Patience is the hardest of all. It helps to recognize that a community is always in process, and it is best to honor and enjoy the process.

Develop a vision and keep developing it. Create glue.

One of the most crucial types of "glue" a group can possess is a clear, shared vision. It is essential for the vision to embody the fundamental nature and deeply felt purpose of the group. It is ideal when every member of the group feels a resounding personal "YES!" in response to it. Keep the vision alive by frequently revisiting it as a group to evaluate whether it still aligns with the group's values.

Build relationships and bonding.

The other fundamental glue for a group comes from the heart. It is crucial to establish solid interpersonal relationships, mutual understanding, compassion, and trust. Doing things together—eating, singing, dancing, telling life stories, traveling, working on projects to help others—facilitates the process much faster than meetings.

Respect different styles.

When the group starts focusing on the tasks that need to be accomplished, personality style conflicts may arise. Some prefer to begin with planning, while others prefer to plunge in and experiment. The challenge for the group as a whole is to get these two tendencies into a constructive relationship so that they contribute to each other. Both are needed.

Maintain balance.

This includes between the group and privately; between doing too much too soon and procrastinating; between physical surroundings and the feeling of community; among qualities of the heart (bonding, caring, trust), the mind (clarity of understanding, vision, integrity), and the will (the ability to act with courage and effectiveness); among different learning and cognitive styles to avoid endless power struggles; and among expenditures—of time as well as money—on current consumption (from food to entertainment), investment (from building to education), and service (which may involve either current consumption or investment).

Get help—to become self-reliant.

It may make sense to depend entirely on outside expertise for some specific topics. For many others, however, it makes sense to cultivate proficiency within the group. Allocate an ample amount of time and resources for group education on accomplishing tasks, managing responsibilities, and building group processes and interpersonal skills. Lack of management or process skills is the number one reason communities fail.

Develop clear procedures.

Creating a community should be an adventure among comrades, not an exercise in bureaucracy, but a little bureaucracy is both necessary and helpful. Specifically, it is prudent to create well-defined, documented procedures for decision-making, conflict resolution, financial management, and membership determination. Perhaps even more important is to create "meta-procedures" for making changes to these (and other) procedures.

Be open and honest.

In numerous community matters, the manner in which we conduct ourselves with transparency and candor is more critical than the action we take. What gets communities into trouble is when the public story no longer fits the private behavior, especially if those in leadership positions are the ones breaking the rules. A healthy approach involves acknowledging what is while also honoring one's principles.[86]

In which ways are you helping to build a closer community around yourself?

10

LEADERSHIP AND MANAGEMENT

"Management is efficiency in climbing the ladder of success; leadership determines whether the ladder is leaning against the right wall."

Stephen Covey

In small or maybe large ways, we are all managers or leaders—of ourselves (see chapter 3), within our families (see chapter 9), and possibly in our work, depending on what we do to make a living and the responsibilities we have in our jobs and careers. This chapter is focused chiefly on organizational management and leadership. It includes comments about management and leadership of projects. I should also say that, at times, we are all also followers. Being a good follower by working hard, being pleasant and upbeat, asking good questions, and making constructive suggestions is also critical to living our lives well. With all these possibilities—as leaders, managers, and followers—we make numerous choices all along the way. These choices have a lot to do with whether or not we thrive.

Throughout our lives, whether we are leading or managing or following—for ourselves, with our families, or within an organization—we have the power to choose how we feel and how we respond to situations, both good and bad. We have the power to make choices about how we live and work in more ways than we realize, and we can make choices about designing our own lives and shaping our work environment. We can thrive in this key dimension of our lives if we choose well.

The words *leadership* and *management* are used interchangeably, but they are very different. Few people are both good leaders and good managers. There are hundreds of books written about leadership and management, but I especially like this simple distinction: a leader does the right things; a manager does things right. Both leading and managing others have a lot to do with effective communication, listening, building trust, empowering others, and establishing a culture where others can perform well.

When it comes to managing, it might be helpful to recognize that there are multiple aspects of managing: we can manage ourselves, we can manage a project, and we can manage a group of people, a department, a company, or an organization. Managing ourselves has a lot to do with developing our personal characteristics, including our habits, becoming disciplined, being prepared and organized, and becoming resilient. It involves becoming trustworthy. These are discussed in chapters 1 and 3.

I have had many leadership and management roles in my life and career. The first of these was in high school, when I was the yearbook editor-in-chief. My high school, Baltimore Polytechnic Institute (Poly), had a long, respected history and was nationally ranked. As a result, becoming the yearbook editor was a serious and daunting task. In my role as leader, among other things, I envisioned something that had never been done before: to add color to selected pages and to operate our budget so that we actually made a profit. After nine months of rigorous work, the final outcome was a resounding success! The management of this was a slightly different story, however. I had eight section editors reporting to me, and each of these editors had from one to three additional staff members. We also had a faculty advisor. My management style left a lot to be desired.

One day early in my tenure, I felt annoyed that there was so much chit-chat going on in our yearbook office that had seemingly nothing to do with getting our work done and our tight deadlines met. So, I decided to put up a sign where all of us could see it, saying, "If you're here to shit, Get!" This had the unintended effect of the staff showing up only to drop off proof pages quickly. I failed to build a culture that was supportive or appreciative. I was not a good listener and was hard-nosed and unforgiving, especially regarding deadlines. Five of the eight section editors started out as personal friends, but by the end of June, only two wanted to socialize with me anymore. This was a very painful experience, and I committed to learning from this by becoming a better manager and continuing to hone my leadership and management skills. Over the next five decades, I have done just that. Today, I consider myself an accomplished and successful leader, and I have dramatically improved my management style and effectiveness. Nevertheless, I am still a better leader than I am a manager, especially as a manager of people.

Over the course of my career, I have read dozens of books and countless articles about management and leadership. The following is a selection of some aspects that stand out most. I hope this chapter will help you and encourage you to be a better leader and manager.

To get the most out of this chapter, I urge you to follow each section by asking yourself:

What kind of leader or manager am I?

How am I doing?

What am I doing well? What can I improve on?

Roles, Traits, Qualities, and Styles

"You don't lead by pointing and telling people some place to go. You lead by going to that place and making a case." Ken Kesey

One central aspect of leadership to understand is what the defining roles are. The well-respected consulting firm McKinsey defines the primary traits of a leader as follows:

- Sets direction. Creates and articulates vision. Frames the issues, often using a written agenda or other visual items.
- Fosters culture. Encourages brainstorming and is open to new ideas. Engages others and sets expectations. Is willing to confront.
- Initiates action. Follows through with persistence. This is sometimes seen as tenacity and determination or, at times, bullheadedness and obstinacy.
- Has the ability to motivate. "If I don't want to, you can't make me. But you can always make me want to."
- Leads by example. A leader brings out the best in others by sharing the best within themselves.

On the other hand, managing is more about these four roles:

- Planning the work
- Organizing the team
- Assigning and directing the work
- Monitoring the result and making adjustments

Are you a leader? Are you a manager? Which of these roles are you playing?

We usually think of leaders as people. If we think of leadership as a person, it's easy to fall into ego and power clashes. I want to suggest another definition of a leader. Consider the leader as the Mission. In this way, different people with different things to contribute at various stages can step forward to guide the rest of the team during the next phase. Of course, with the leader-as-Mission approach, the roles and traits described here will be required when we step forward for a period to lead or manage.

Great leaders inspire action. In a TED Talk,[87] Simon Sinek suggests we start with why, not how—because people might not do things the way we do, but they respond to why we do them. He recommends we consider the Golden Circle, comprising three concentric circles. The outer ring is about *what*. The middle circle is about *how*. The innermost circle is about *why*. Great leaders go from the inside circle outward. They inspire others by saying, "We believe in *x*, *y*, and *z*; therefore, let's do *a*, *b*, and *c*. Doing business with people who believe what we believe enhances our effectiveness, creates loyalty, and forms culture.

To be a leader requires certain qualities in today's world. Consider these four:

Brains—deep knowledge of their area of work. Knowledge, expertise, and ideas are valued.

Soul—clear values. Leaders drive to true north, pursuing what's right, not what's expedient. They lead with a moral compass.

Heart—passion and compassion. These are essential motivators, helping drive toward goals and basing decisions on concern for others.

Good nerves—Leaders must be bold and able to move toward their vision, even with incomplete information, changing events, or risky odds.

Another view of the essential qualities of a leader, developed by Warren Bennis, a pioneer in leadership studies, suggests that the leader needs to have a vision; a commitment to excellence; belief in people and teamwork; virtue along with a moral compass; boundless enthusiasm; willingness to take risks; devotion to long-term growth rather than short-term profit; readiness; endless curiosity; and overall, a broad education.[88]

Which qualities do you have? What are you strong in? What needs attention?

Regarding styles of leadership, an article in *Forbes* magazine[89] described these:

Visionary—Apple's Steve Jobs and Whole Foods' John Mackey are examples. Their vision, the quality of their products, and their brand are all closely intertwined.

Empathetic—Bill Hewlett, the cofounder of Hewlett-Packard, was a legendary one. He liked to inspire engineers by walking the floors and listening to their ideas and concerns. Empathetic leadership under founder Herb Kelleher is why Southwest Airlines flight attendants are among the most content in the industry.

Humble servitude—demonstrated by Walmart chairman S. Robson Walton. He said the job of leaders is to "listen to customers, listen to customers, listen to customers," and in doing so, create a culture of service throughout the organization.

Moral/ethical—Companies like SC Johnson, Deere & Co., American Express, and Starbucks have done well by doing good. Insisting on ethical behavior throughout the company by having employees abide by the Golden Rule in their interactions with colleagues and customers can be a powerful form of leadership. As Mary Waldrop said, "It's important that people know what you stand for. It's equally important that they know what you won't stand for." Cautionary note: This leadership style is also fragile and subject to human frailty. One mistake and the moral/ethical leader can quickly look like a hypocrite. As a result, you must walk the walk, not just talk the talk.

What is your leadership style?

The Covey Leadership Center has another framework for leadership. They consider the four levels of principle-centered leadership to be as follows:

Level	Focus	Key Principle
1. Personal	Self	Trustworthiness
2. Interpersonal	People	Trust
3. Managerial	Style, skills	Empowerment
4. Organizational	Shared vision and principles, structure, systems, strategy	Alignment

Which levels are you focusing on?

To get things done as a leader or as a manager, we have to use power effectively. Part of our power depends on how much we can control ourselves and how much we impact others. We can use our power to make things happen and to influence events, outcomes, and conversations. Power comes from a variety of things, including our physical presence (being tall or attractive, for example), our voice (tone and loudness, for example), our degree of articulateness, and certainly our personality. Abraham Lincoln said, "Most anyone can stand adversity, but to test a man's character give him power." There are generally thought to be six sources of power:

Reward—Give people what they want.

Coercion—Use fear to get people to do what we want.

Information—Know something relevant and important that others don't.

Legitimacy—Hold an acknowledged position of authority. Formal: a CEO, as an example. Informal: a parent, for example.

Expertise—Have knowledge of subject matter; for example, being the only engineer in the company.

Reverence—Possess fame, status, charisma; people respect or admire us and follow us.

Which power do you have and use?

Given all the above, it might be valuable to evaluate yourself as a leader along a set of continuums developed by Burke Miller. Rank yourself from 1 to 10 in each category below:

<u>**Identity and purpose:**</u> From no clue to crystal clear. Do you know what you are here for? Are you clearly connected to your

purpose, vision, Spirit, and higher self? Do you understand how your specific abilities and interests align with what the world needs? Do you have clear values that you stand for?

Worldview: From limiting to empowering. Does how you see yourself, others, and the world enable or hinder you and those around you? Does how you see things help create the kind of world you want to live in? Are you open-minded and aware of your beliefs? Do you understand that the ability to embrace conflicting perspectives is an example of an empowering way of looking at the world?

Integrity: From zip to total. This is about how you are to yourself and others. Do you keep your commitments to yourself and others? Do your actions and choices align with your purpose? Rank two aspects on the continuum: separately rank **Honesty** and **Authenticity** (being true to your own personality and living your life according to your own values and goals).

Empowering relationships: From shut down to opened up. In your relationships, do you create opportunities for collaboration and encourage others to share their talents, interests, and unique qualities? Do you exhibit vulnerability, openheartedness, whole-heartedness, and emotional awareness? Do you acknowledge and appreciate others? Do you look for the best in others? Do you handle conflict as an opportunity to arrive at creative solutions?[90]

How do you assess yourself on these continuums? Specifically, what can you do to improve?

Reciprocal Relationships

"Abundance is a dance with reciprocity—what we can give, what we can share, and what we receive in the process." Terry Tempest Williams

Leadership (and, to a large extent, management) is a reciprocal relationship between those who choose to lead and those who decide to follow. The essential aspect of a leader is that they have followers. Any discussion of leadership must attend to the dynamics of this relationship. Strategies, tactics, skills, and practices are empty unless we connect leaders to the people they lead. If there is no underlying need for the relationship, then there is no need for leaders. Note: Throughout this section, I'll refer to leaders, but in many cases, these points apply to managers as well.

The key to working effectively with others is building relationships. It all starts with our relationship with ourselves. We have to go beyond our ego. We have to overcome our fear. Then we need to model leadership, which can be done in numerous ways, including thanking people, listening well, and sharing something personal about ourselves. And instead of simply announcing a conclusion, which can be difficult for people to digest, we can model leadership by walking through the process and why. These can create vulnerability and take courage.

The old approach to leading and managing was command and control. Top-down. The new approach is to seek to connect. To develop people and have them follow us, we must be connected to them. Truly connecting means we need to have a passionate commitment to their ability. We need to listen to others for their frame of reference, which affirms and respects them. We need to listen with the intent to replay. To be effective, be a sponge, listen, and ask questions. The paradox of listening is that by relinquishing power—the temporary power of speaking, asserting, and knowing— we become more powerful. And be sure to engage in dialogue rather than debate (see chapter 9).

To achieve success, we must develop people and our relationships with them. There are several vital elements to this. The first key to connecting in relationships is appreciating and accepting differences. This leads to synergy—when the combined effect is greater than the sum of the separate actions—and synergy often enhances our effectiveness and overall outcomes. Secondly, our people have to believe us and buy into what we are saying. Our credibility and competency contribute to buy-in. To create buy-in, we must generate believe-in by valuing others' opinions, not telling them everything to do, and letting them contribute.

In what ways are you connecting? How are you building synergy, buy-in, and believe-in? What could you do better or more of?

Relationships also require trust. Trust is the conduit of influence. Building trust means taking risks. Telling the truth is indispensable. If someone we're trying to influence doesn't trust us, we're not going to get very far. We might even elicit suspicion because we come across as manipulative. We might have great ideas, but those ideas can fall flat without trust. A warm, trustworthy person who is also strong elicits admiration, but only after we have established trust does our strength become a gift rather than a threat.

Another critical aspect of building trust is admitting an error when we were wrong. We must own up to times when we are wrong and do what we can to fix what we did. Mistakes and failures expose our vulnerabilities, making us uncomfortable. Depending on the situation, we might need to apologize. These all take courage and humility but often result in our being more trusted.

What are you doing to build trust? With whom? With whom are you not building trust?

When we are wrong or make an error, it will help to remember that a mistake can become an opportunity when we do something about it. In general, bad news can become good news. I learned this the hard way. My first job after college was as a systems analyst. Early on, I created a complex software program (using key-punched cards). I excitedly returned the following day to see the main CDC 6400 computer printout. Line 3 showed that the program had been aborted due to errors in coding I had made. Dejectedly, I returned to my office, but along the way, Jerry, a senior programmer, saw my discouraged face and asked what was wrong. When I explained, he laughed! I was furious (on top of being dejected) until he said this bad news was actually good news because now I could learn (with his kind help) how to code correctly.

Habits for Success and Best Practices

"The elevator to success is out of order. You'll have to use the stairs . . . one step at a time." Joe Girard

By creating and following specific habits and best practices, employees, managers, leaders, and the organization overall are more likely to succeed and thrive. What habits and best practices are these? After reviewing many important, large projects, Warren Bennis discovered that leaders of successful projects habitually do these things: They are willing to abandon their ego for the talents of others—they become curators, not creators. They recruit meticulously. They always remind people why we're here—it's about the project. They form groups that are not hierarchical. Great groups make great leaders. Considering these four habits, it's not surprising that the projects led to success![91]

For us to be successful and prosper, more often than not, we need to be interdependent in our work with others. Three excellent habits for being interdependent are set out in *The 7 Habits of Highly Effective People*. (Note: Habits 1, 2, and 3, about being independent and gaining self-mastery, are discussed in chapter 3 of *Thriving!*). As shown below, habits 4, 5, and 6 are:

4. **Think win-win.** This is about creating mutually beneficial outcomes in all our interactions.

5. **Seek first to understand, then to be understood.** This habit is about actively seeking to understand and communicate the other person's perspective first. Once we've done that, we can express our own thoughts and concerns.

6. **Synergize.** Habit 6 emphasizes searching for and appreciating the opinions, views, and perspectives of others to generate better solutions than we would have come up with individually.[92]

Which of these habits are you following? How are you leading or managing in an interdependent way? What more could you be doing?

One of the most challenging habits for people, especially in the early part of their careers, is to "manage up." This means that we have a responsibility to ourselves to work with our boss or bosses to communicate how we see things, what we need in order to be more effective, and when and why we are struggling—either because the tasks are too difficult or the deadlines too short or because of some interpersonal issues. We are responsible for helping to shape our work environment. Don't assume your boss or bosses know what you know. Nor do you know what they know. Ask them for clarity.

Help to manage their expectations. Be constructive throughout. It will help to think through (consider writing a draft) and present what you want to say and the one or two main points you want to be sure your boss understands. Consider this as a source of strength. Good bosses will respect you for managing up. By the way, much of this also applies to child-parent relationships.

Related to managing up is advocating for ourselves. This includes several things, including speaking up when we need assistance and asking questions if we don't understand or we need clarification. It includes helping teachers and bosses gain a more complete understanding of what is happening to us, giving them our perspective. My wife and I learned about this in spades when our son, who has hearing loss, was in grammar school. Obviously, we couldn't be with him at school. He had to learn to advocate for himself, often asking the teacher to face the class and repeat what was just said. My wife helped the school and the teachers by handing out a list of best practices, but the primary responsibility for hearing what was going on and being treated well was on his shoulders. Fortunately, he became very adept at this.

Are you being effective in managing up and advocating for yourself? Give examples. What could you do better?

In terms of best practices, three of my favorite descriptions of best management and leadership principles are:

"Six Habits of Extraordinary Bosses," by Geoffrey James https://business.time.com/2012/09/27/6-habits-of-extraordinary-bosses/

"The 8 Core Beliefs of Extraordinary Bosses," by Geoffrey James

https://www.inc.com/geoffrey-james/8-core-beliefs-of-extraordinary-bosses.html

"10 Thoughts about Leadership," by Jon Gordon

https://jongordon.com/positive-tip-leadership-thoughts.html

My distillation of these three fabulous pieces of advice follows, grouped into four key aspects: role and style, vision, culture, and process. With reference to the three sources listed above, I have noted each point below as derived from either Geoffrey James ("GJSix" or "GJ8," respectively) or Jon Gordon ("JG10"). I wish I had followed these pieces of advice more closely in my career!

About Role and Style

Leadership is not just about what we do but what we can inspire, encourage, and empower others to do. (JG10)

Trust is the force that connects people to the leader and their vision. If people trust their leader, they will work toward the vision. (JG10)

Let people do their jobs. Provide coaching only when necessary or if requested. (GJSix)

A manager's job is to ask the questions that spark the thought processes and ideas that will make that employee successful. Ask questions rather than give answers. (GJSix)

Invest in your people and develop a relationship with them. Otherwise, they will underperform or rebel. (JG10)

About Vision

A company is a collection of individual hopes and dreams, all connected to a higher purpose. (GJ8)

Motivation comes from vision, not from fear. Employees work harder because they believe in the organization's goals, enjoy what they're doing, and know how they'll share in the rewards. (GJ8)

People follow the leader first and the leader's vision second. If the leader is not someone people will follow, the vision will never be realized. (JG10)

About Culture

Leaders inspire and teach their people to focus on solutions, not complaints. Lead with optimism, enthusiasm, and positive energy. Weed out negativity and guard against pessimism (JG10).

Avoid creating superstars. Coordinate individual goals so that they intersect with and support team goals. Compensate based on how the team (rather than just the individual) performs and encourage top performers to use their talents to create a broader level of success. (GJSix)

Remove the nonperformers. Monitor employee performance and provide constructive coaching when an employee falls short. However, once it's clear that a person can't perform, either reassign that employee to a more appropriate job or suggest finding a job elsewhere. (GJSix)

The best way to please investors, peers, and customers is to put the employees first. Employees create, build, sell, and support the products that customers buy, thereby creating investor value (and helping advance a manager's career). (GJSix)

Expect excellence everywhere. To get there, treat every employee as the most valuable person in the organization. (GJ8)

Create teams that adapt easily to new markets and can quickly form partnerships with other companies, customers, and possibly even competitors. (GJ8)

Make work fun, not mere toil. The most important job of a manager is, as far as possible, to put people in positions that they can enjoy. (GJ8)

About Process

Success is a process, not a destination. Winning is the by-product of outstanding leadership, teamwork, focus, commitment, and execution of the fundamentals. As a leader, focus on your people and process, not the outcome. (JG10)

Manage people, not numbers. Numbers represent only the history of what's happened. The best way to have great numbers is to ensure that the job gets done. Manage people and their activities so that the numbers take care of themselves. (GJSix)

Set a general direction and then commit to obtaining the resources employees need to complete the job. Push decision-making downward, allowing teams to form their own rules, and intervene only in emergencies. (GJ8)

Technology offers empowerment, not automation. Using technology is a way to free human beings to be creative and build better relationships. Adapt back-office systems to the tools that people actually want to use. (GJ8)

Change is an inevitable part of life. Success is possible only if employees and organizations embrace new ideas and ways of doing business. (GJ8)

SECTION III
THRIVING IN THE WORLD

"Let yours be a voice for the rivers
Let yours be a voice for the forests
Let yours be a voice for the desert
Let yours be a voice for the oceans
Let yours be a voice for the children
Let yours be a voice for the dreamer
Let yours be a voice of no regret."

David Whyte

Thriving in the World

11 - Charity, Philanthropy, and Service

- *Being Generous with Our Money*
- *Using Our Time and Talents*
- *Serving on Boards and Committees*

12 - Conservation and the Environment

- *Liking and Caring about the Natural World*
- *Important Choices We Can Make*
- *Our Planet Needs Our Help*

11

CHARITY, PHILANTHROPY, AND SERVICE

"Life's most persistent and urgent question is 'What are you doing for others?' "

Martin Luther King Jr.

Giving generously of our time, talents, and money is likely to help bring about desirable changes in the world—such as solving some of society's pervasive social and economic problems, encouraging the arts, supporting education at various levels, and preserving natural resources. As Os Guinness writes in *Long Journey Home: A Guide to Your Search for the Meaning of Life*, "Remember that nothing gives power and energy like a worthy purpose, and a worthy purpose always has something to do with being generous with your time, money, and love."[93] Doing so helps us thrive.

Being Generous with Our Money

"We make a living by what we get. We make a life by what we give." Sir Winston Churchill

Both *charity* and *philanthropy* can mean taking action in the spirit of caring and generosity to address the needs of others and the planet. Charity is commonly understood as the direct transfer of resources, typically money, with the intent of helping those in immediate need. Charity may be regarded as a temporary solution to a current problem. On the other hand, philanthropy is generally understood as giving that will encourage self-improvement and social empowerment. Philanthropy need not be defined by the size of the gift and may extend beyond sharing money to include making gifts of time, effort, and expertise.

Are you charitable? Philanthropic? Which problems are of most concern to you?

Ultimately, our ideas about giving and the expression of our charitable or philanthropic intent will be rooted in our values and expectations for how our generosity can make a difference. To achieve desired change, we need to continue learning, studying, and preparing to use our knowledge and wisdom in our compassionate work.

According to the medieval philosopher Maimonides, there is an eight-step hierarchy of values when it comes to charity, each one higher than the one before:

1. The first and lowest rung on the ladder is to give grudgingly, reluctantly, or with regret.

2. The second is to give less than one should but with grace.

3. The third is to give what one should but only after being asked.

4. The fourth is to give before one is asked.

5. Number five is to give without knowing who will receive it; only the recipient knows the giver's identity.

6. Number six is to give anonymously, but knowing who the recipient is.

7. Seven is to give so that neither the giver nor the receiver knows the identity of the other.

8. The eighth and highest level of giving is to help someone to become self-reliant.

Which level of charity do you pursue? What will it take for you to move to higher levels?

As you engage in being generous, consider focusing your giving on addressing the root causes of problems, not just their symptoms. These root causes are the attitudes, decisions, and events that give rise to and are ultimately responsible for the difficulties and problems confronting us. They include such attitudes as greed, arrogance, self-centeredness, unchangeable opinions and judgments, lack of compassion, excessive materialism and competitiveness, and short-sightedness.

Even if you don't have significant wealth, you can still be charitable or philanthropic. There are many good articles on the Internet about this and ideas about how much to give. You can start with 1 percent of your annual income and work your way up. For some people, it might help to make contributions weekly or monthly. You can research to see what percentage would be needed if you want to match the charitable donations of the average American in your income bracket (for example, 2017 AGI data indicates it's 7 percent for those earning between $30,000 and $50,000, and 5 percent for those earning between $50,000 and $100,000). Keep in mind that charitable contributions are tax deductible under current law.

Those who have earned their wealth through their own talents and efforts find their lives significantly enriched by engaging in philanthropic activities. And for someone who inherits substantial wealth, other than choosing good parents, it's often thought that the best thing that can happen to them is to become philanthropically involved.

Helping our children toward this life emphasis is also an important aspect of being charitable or philanthropic. We can teach them its importance, for as the great coach John Wooden said, "You can't live a perfect day without doing something for someone who will never be able to repay you." We can encourage our children with these values through our personal examples and teaching. Parents can choose to distribute some of their philanthropic funds to their children before their own deaths, helping their offspring learn firsthand how to manage their money and give it in the best way. It's valuable to allow children to make mistakes and turn them into learning opportunities.

And beyond our families, our charity and philanthropy can influence people we know and those we don't know, as well as those with power and influence.

Are you teaching your children to be charitable or philan-thropic? In what ways? What more can you do to ensure that they pursue this in their own lives? In what ways are you influencing others?

Ever since my wife and I were married, we have annually sat down to discuss to whom and how much we would make philanthropic contributions. When we were 50 years old, we set up a donor-advised fund, which has been very easy to use. When we are no longer able, our plan is for our children to be responsible for directing the annual contributions. Since our annual contributions are not enormous by certain standards, it helps to have more impact by having a focus. After carefully doing our research to determine the organizations' effectiveness, we intentionally make donations to only approximately a dozen different organizations each year.

Jim Morgan advises donating to organizations that have these characteristics:

- Effective leadership with a clear and ambitious vision and a well-designed plan for implementation.
- A clear mission that spells out the organization's objectives for the next five years, and the reasons behind them.
- A culture of transparency in terms of financial information, program assessment, results, and impact.
- Strong partnerships with their board, donors, volunteers, other nonprofits, businesses, and government.[94]

One of the criteria my family believes in is requiring the money received by the organization to be spent primarily on programs and not on overhead, which includes marketing and executive salaries and benefits. Specifically, we require organizations we support to spend no more than 20 percent of their annual income on overhead. Several websites help with this research, including www.guidestar.org, www.charitynavigator.org, and www.justgiving.com.

Using Our Time and Talents

"Everybody can be great, because everybody can serve."
Martin Luther King Jr.

There are myriad ways to use our time and talents to help others and the natural world. Rolling up our sleeves and lending a helping hand by using our time and talents to help others and organizations we believe in, as well as the land, water, air, animals, and plants around us, can be important and beneficial in numerous ways. Our involvement can be national or international, but often the most impact and connection we can have is local. It starts by reflecting on the world we live in and seeing what's needed. To have the most impact, it's best to get involved in something you care about, and something you already know about and have experience with or insight into. You don't have to be an expert at the beginning; you can learn along the way. You just need to bring your energy, care, and enthusiasm. I love what Ruth Bader Ginsburg, the late Supreme Court justice, wrote: "Fight for the things you care about, but do it in a way that will lead others to join you."

Using our time and talents can contribute to building stronger and healthier neighborhoods, schools, and hometowns. Here's a summary of more local opportunities:

- With our neighbors, schools, kids' sports, Boy and Girl Scouts, and the elderly, as well as work as citizens in local government

- With groups we belong to, including religious organizations (see chapter 6) and civic organizations such as Rotary, Kiwanis, and Lions Clubs
- With people locally or far away who need our help, whether financially, with their health, or in receiving an education
- Helping our planet also contributes to the possibility of a healthier ecosystem for us and the next generations (see chapter 12). We can be involved with beach and park cleanups and local and national organizations such as the Sierra Club, which offer volunteer opportunities on an ongoing or project basis. My wife and I have enjoyed doing this for the past 15 years!

And by helping others, we are helping ourselves. Giving to others helps us be grateful for what we have and gives us meaningful purpose (see chapters 7 and 8). Selfishly, it could be argued that by serving others, there's a better chance we'll be taken care of when we need something. What goes around comes around.

What issues are most important to you? Which organizations are you volunteering for? Which one will you consider using your time and talents with?

Of course, depending on your level of commitment, getting involved can be very time-consuming. But it doesn't have to be. You can have a meaningful impact without spending much time. You can contribute even if you only attend a meeting every few weeks, speak up, and otherwise participate. It is essential to know your limits and schedules and be able to say no.

What will it take for you to make the time and get involved? Consider making a plan with people who can encourage you, support you, and give you good advice.

I love the poem "To Be of Use," by Marge Piercy,[95] with so many images of people working to do what needs to be done:

> *The people I love the best jump into work head first*
> *Without dallying in the shallows and swim off*
> *with sure strokes almost out of sight.*
> *. . . the thing worth doing well done has a shape that satisfies,*
> *clean and evident.*

Serving on Boards and Committees

"A good Board of Directors team is one where ideas are flowing fluidly—and where each idea is met with an initial welcome, an intellectual challenge, an expression of gratitude, a rigorous scrutiny and a readiness for action." Hendrith Vanlon Smith Jr.

Besides volunteering, we can also serve on boards, advisory boards, and committees. Usually, people are invited onto boards and committees because of a need for specific knowledge and experience. In some cases, such as a city's opera or symphony, well-known people who can make significant financial contributions are sought. In all cases, boards and committees need people who support the mission and have valuable thoughts to share. This applies to achieving progress on all boards and committees.

Be aware that there are distinctly different kinds of boards. This needs to be better understood so that we don't think we are on the board for a different reason than the board, CEO, or executive director wants. My experience suggests that there are five different kinds of boards:

1. **Service boards**, such as boards of alumni, where there is little or no external funding or staff. The work and funding are fundamentally done by the members of the local board, who run events and might charge an admission fee.

2. **Fundraising boards**, such as for an opera or symphony, where the principal value of the board is pledging funds personally, being willing to contact their friends and business clients, and allowing their names to be used.

3. **Fiduciary boards**, such as a public utility board, where the board, through its committees, certifies things like financial statements and other critical audits such as safety.

4. **Cheerleading boards**, where the organization's management is capable and effective, or at least thinks of itself that way. The power in the organization is concentrated in the CEO or executive director and their executive team, with the board essentially acting as a sounding board and often a rubber stamp. The board's purpose is to support the management, with generally little in the way of serious discussion or constructive criticism invited.

5. **Generative, policy, and strategy boards**, which focus on the organization's central purpose, mission, strategy, and key policies. On such boards, discussion and the use of outside experts can be extensive. The management team prepares detailed materials for the board's review, often at the specific request of the board. School boards and city councils would be examples.

A great book about nonprofits and their boards is *Governance as Leadership*, by Richard Chait, William Ryan, and Barbara Taylor.[96] It goes into great detail, with many excellent examples of the different types of boards described above. **Will you consider serving on a board or committee? Which kind of board or committee is most attractive to you?**

If you are on a board, what kind of board is it? Is there alignment with what you offer?

Board Search Partners suggested eight questions to answer before joining a board of directors. These questions, whether the board is for a for-profit or not-for-profit organization, are:

<u>Will you be passionate about this organization?</u>

Honestly, do you find the organization really interesting to you?

<u>Can you devote enough time?</u>

To be a valuable member of the board, it is important to have the availability to attend all meetings and ensure that the board's schedule does not clash with yours.

<u>Is this a team you want to join?</u>

Make sure to meet all members of the board, as well as the CEO or executive director, CFO, and general counsel. Check references for the CEO or executive director and board members, and ensure that they possess the highest level of quality and integrity.

<u>Can you add real value?</u>

Verify that you have a solid understanding of the organization, including its current and potential markets, its competitors, and the products and services it offers. Make sure your skills and talents offer genuine value and are needed.

Do the financials hold up to scrutiny?

Review recent annual and quarterly reports and other required governmental filings. If you don't know how to interpret these, get help improving your financial acumen immediately.

Does this organization have a good chance of success?

Evaluate the organization thoroughly by considering the current and future challenges it may face, and determine whether the board and officers have the capability and willingness to address them.

Are you protected from any liability?

Confirm that the organization offers sufficient Directors and Officers (D&O) insurance. Ask if it provides director indemnification. Check your personal umbrella policy. Then have your attorney review all these.

Will you get a good return on your investment?

If it's important to you, assess whether joining the organization will provide you with opportunities to gain new knowledge, build professional connections, and further your career. And, possibly more important, consider whether serving could support your purpose as a person (see chapter 8).

Based on my experience with boards over four decades, I would add the following to this list. It's important to listen, keep learning, and offer the best of yourself. It's best to join boards with people who sincerely welcome your input. Some boards are comfortable with how things have been and resist anything that feels like it's rocking the boat. If they're not open to new suggestions or are not listening, you could be wasting your time and become frustrated. But don't be arrogant. Remember the Serenity Prayer: "God, grant me the serenity to accept the things I cannot change, the courage to change the things I can, and the wisdom to know the difference." Finally, many boards change their board members very seldom, regardless of what is stated in their by-laws. Once you have made a contribution to the board, and if you have served several years (check the by-laws, but generally, I think serving for five years is about the right amount of time), or if you are not able to advise the board effectively, then move on.

As you consider joining a board or committee, keep in mind that some organizations attempt to make things happen by changing the established approach to the issues or creating something entirely new. This can be pretty challenging. As Machiavelli wrote in *The Prince*, "There is nothing more difficult to carry out, nor more doubtful of success, nor more dangerous to handle, than to initiate a new order of things." Social change is highly complex. Here are a few points from Krista Tippett about what we have learned about how social change happens:

- You can catch more flies with honey than with vinegar.
- People in the center are not going to initiate big changes.
- To make change, you must put yourself at the margins and be willing to risk.
- You have to approach differences with the belief that there is good in the other.[97]

With this in mind, I highly recommend reading *Power and Love: A Theory and Practice of Social Change*, which does a fabulous job of discussing what's involved in creating social change. The author, Adam Kahane, says that employing power and love is like learning to walk on two legs. (In his metaphor, one leg is power, and the other is love.) The trick is to shift from one leg to the other and stay in balance without falling or stumbling. When we get good at this, we can go faster and faster, and even run.

12

CONSERVATION AND THE ENVIRONMENT

"As we and our land are part of one another, so all who are living as neighbors here, human and plant and animal, are part of one another, and so cannot possibly flourish alone."

Wendell Berry

There is a direct connection between being in nature and personally thriving. I subscribe to the broader set of reasons for being in nature and caring about nature discussed below. I hope you do too!

Animals, plants, and Mother Earth can thrive too. This, however, will require our help and changes to patterns of human life that are now firmly under way. Much has been written about extinction, global warming and its impacts, and policy and tax methods to deal with our environmental challenges. I encourage you to become more informed and engaged in these matters.

Liking and Caring about the Natural World

"In wilderness is the preservation of the world." *Henry David Thoreau*[98]

To see how valuable nature and green space are to people, check out where they want to live: near parks, trees, flowers, and bushes, and near rivers, lakes, oceans, and mountains. With these things in mind, I especially like what Alice Walker wrote:

> *"We have a beautiful mother,*
>
> *Her green lap immense, . . .*
>
> *Her blue body everything we know."*

People cite many reasons why they like to be in nature, including:

- It's fun; we can relax and be happy. One of the greatest environmentalist US presidents, Theodore Roosevelt, said, "There is a delight in the hearty life of the open."
- There is a quietness and a calm that can come from being in nature.
- It can be restorative and rejuvenating.
- It's good for personal health.
- We can learn new things—about animals and plants, or skills for hiking, camping, and the like.
- In nature, we can enjoy using all five of our senses.
- There, we can enjoy sheer beauty.

- We can connect with our sense of gratitude.
- Seeing something grand or beautiful can be humbling, even spiritual, for some people. "Even stones have a love, a love that seeks the ground" (Meister Eckhart).

Why do you like to be in nature?

There are many reasons posited for why we might care about our planet. These include:

- Everything is interrelated. Humans cannot survive without a healthy planet to live on. Daniel Quinn cleverly said, "Without Swiss cheese, what is the hole? Without man, what is the gorilla? Without the gorilla, what is man?"
- Animals and plants—not only humans—have a form of intelligence.
- If not us humans, who will speak for the animals?
- Nature provides enormous ecosystem services, like clean water and fresh air.
- There is significant fragility now, including extinctions and global warming.
- We can fill a much-needed role as stewards to conserve, protect, and restore.

In which ways do you care about the natural world? Why?

Important Choices We Can Make

"Our challenge is keeping affluence under control. This doesn't mean everyone gets poorer. It means everyone gets enough and stops." Donella Meadows[99]

There are numerous ways we impact our planet. Some of these are helpful, but unfortunately, many are harmful. To survive and create a healthy world, we must take individual responsibility for creating an ecologically sustainable world. As re-created by Ted Perry in 1972, Chief Seattle so eloquently said, "The Earth does not belong to man. Man belongs to the Earth. Man did not weave the web of life. He is merely a strand in it. Whatever he does to the web, he does to himself."

Many people would argue that nature is here to serve us. They calculate the value of land and other resources based primarily on economics, which often focuses on short-term considerations. This, however, leads to many problems. One of our early foremost environmentalists, Aldo Leopold, who wrote *A Sand County Almanac*, explained, "We abuse land because we regard it as a commodity belonging to us. When we see land as a community to which we belong, we may be able to use it with love and respect."[100]

Overall, our lifestyles in the developed world lead to considerable consumption. This requires resource extraction and adds to pollution. Robert Muller[101] wrote, "The single most important contribution any of us can make to the planet is to return to frugality." Don't worry! This does not mean that we have to become hermits wearing worn-out clothes, but it does mean we have to learn to live with limits.

There is an overall approach we can take to limit our environmental impacts, which I call the seven Rs. They are:

Reduce

Reuse

Reclaim

Recycle

Redesign

Rent

Resist impulse purchases, purchasing items that are not energy efficient

Which of these are you doing regularly? What could you do more of?

And there are many specific things we can do, some of which are pretty doable if we commit to them. Here are 10 things I hope you'll consider doing:

1. Consume less. See the discussion of "enoughness" in chapter 4.
2. Confirm that purchases are nontoxic, energy efficient, long-lived, simply packaged, or unpackaged.
3. When considering making a gift, ask if it honors ecological values.
4. Adopt a species.
5. Plant trees.
6. Carry your own bags to the grocery store.
7. Run your life so that you have only one bag of garbage a week. Compost.
8. Eat organic foods whenever economically feasible.

9. Conserve water—take timed and shorter showers; have plants and lawns that need little water.

10. Make more purchases of used items, borrow things from friends and neighbors, and rent when possible.

Which of these are you doing? What other helpful things are you doing?

The good news is that today people are paying vastly more attention to environmental sustainability. *Sustainability* has emerged as a term that goes beyond environmentalism and conservation issues. Sustainability inherently means going from parts to the whole. It involves thoughtful design, embodies fairness and equity, and can lead to building a stronger sense of community. According to Andres Edwards, sustainability encompasses the following four broad, inter-related aspects of life—what some people call the three Es plus one:[102]

Environment/Ecology

Economy/Employment

Equality/Social Equity

Education

We need to make progress in all of these areas in order to achieve sustainability. We can choose to pursue the four aspects of sustainability in both our private and public lives.

There are many other ways we can support the health of our planet. Some people think that business will provide goods and services that embody sustainability. This is based partly on the view so well expressed by Paul Hawken, author of *The Ecology of Commerce: A Declaration of Sustainability*. He said, "Business is the only mechanism on the planet today powerful enough to produce the changes necessary to reverse global environmental and social degradation." New technology is also thought to provide crucial solutions.

Do you agree with this? If so, in what ways? If not, why not?

Another approach is joining and donating to environmental organizations. Some of these are local, others national, and still others international. One of these is the National Wildlife Federation, which has been uniting Americans for more than 85 years to ensure that wildlife thrives in our changing world. The federation pulls together people from across the United States in both solidarity and action to protect and conserve America's natural heritage. It was founded on the following core beliefs:

- Our nation's wildlife, healthy waters, clean air, and public lands are the birthright of all Americans.
- Our nation's thriving lakes, rivers, streams, wetlands, marine and coastal waters, forests, and other wild lands are vital to our public health, economy, wildlife, and quality of life.
- Diverse and abundant wildlife habitat is essential for urban, suburban, and rural communities.
- We all have the right to enjoy sustainable and responsible outdoor recreation, including hunting, fishing, camping, birding, wildlife watching, hiking, climbing, swimming, boating, gardening, or simply basking in the beauty of nature.
- We have a national responsibility to get our children outdoors for their health, intellectual enrichment, and daily happiness and to instill a conservation ethic in future generations.

We can also be champions for our environment in public policy. This includes supporting ballot proposals and candidates for public office who are environmentally conscious. Consider the Sierra Club's Environmental Bill of Rights, which follows:

Every American has the right to a safe and healthy environment. We support the following simple principles and hold public officials who represent us accountable for their stewardship of the planet:

- Prevent Pollution. Every American is entitled to air, water, food, and communities free from toxic chemicals. Government policies and regulatory standards must prevent pollution before it happens, expand citizens' right to know about toxics, and guarantee protection for citizens, particularly for the most vulnerable among us—infants, children, pregnant women, and the elderly.

- Preserve America's National Heritage wild and beautiful for our children and future generations. Wildlife, forests, mountains, prairies, wetlands, rivers, lakes, historic sites, urban parks, open spaces, oceans, and coastlines are all part of our national heritage.

- Conserve America's National Resources by controlling waste, increasing energy efficiency, and protecting against overuse and abuse. Encourage sustainable technologies that meet human needs without destroying the environment.

- End the Giveaways of Public Assets such as mineral, timber, grazing, and fishery resources. End the subsidies for oil and energy companies. Polluters should pay to clean up any mess they create. No one has the right to use property in a way that destroys or degrades the surrounding community. We reject the idea that good neighbors must pay bad ones not to pollute.

- Get the Big Money out of Politics. No more government for sale. Let's take back our government from the big campaign contributors and exploiters who control it today.

Which parts of this Bill of Rights do you support? What would you add or change?

Humboldt State University (California) students initiated the Graduation Pledge of Social and Environmental Responsibility almost 25 years ago. Today, it is widely accepted throughout the US and in many other countries. It states: "*I pledge to explore and take into account the social and environmental consequences of any job I consider and will try to improve these aspects of any organizations for which I work.*"

Students define for themselves what it means to be socially and environmentally responsible. Students at over a hundred colleges and universities have used the pledge at some level. The schools involved include small liberal arts colleges (including Colgate and Macalester), large state universities (such as Oregon and Utah), and large private research universities (including the University of Pennsylvania, Stanford, and Duke). The pledge is also now found at graduate and professional schools, in high schools, and overseas (Taiwan and Australia).

Graduates who voluntarily signed the pledge have turned down jobs with which they did not feel morally comfortable and have worked to make changes once on the job. For example, they have promoted recycling at their organizations, removed racist language from a training manual, worked for gender parity in high school athletics, and helped to convince an employer to refuse a chemical-weapons-related contract.

In a sense, the pledge operates at three levels: *students* making choices about their employment; *schools* educating about values and citizenship rather than only knowledge and skills; and the *workplace and society* being concerned about more than just the bottom line. The impact is immense, even if only a significant minority of the one million college graduates sign and live out the pledge each year.

What are your thoughts about signing this pledge or encouraging a graduating college senior to sign it?

Our Planet Needs Our Help

"We believe that interest in nature leads to knowledge, which is followed by understanding and, later, appreciation. Once respect is gained, it is a short step to responsibility, and ultimately, action—to preserve our earth." The Wilderness Leadership School

A considerable amount has been written about the condition of our planet and the crises it is facing. All of these affect us humans too. We have choices and decisions to make. Our culture is at the heart of many of these challenges. While we are making progress in some ways, the processes that guide our lives are well established and entrenched. We are running out of time. The Foundation for Conscious Evolution wrote this a few years ago:

> *For billions of years, life has evolved unconsciously through a process of natural selection. Now, suddenly, in our lifetime, we find that we are affecting our own evolution by everything we do: the number of babies we have; the food we eat; the cars we drive; the way we build, fight and endure. Through the development of science and technology, we understand the invisible technologies of creation: the gene, the atom, the brain. We can now destroy our world or restore the Earth, free people from hunger, emancipate human creativity,*

and explore the further regions of the human spirit and the universe beyond our planet. Within this living generation, we must become capable of ethical and wise guidance of the process of evolution by human selection and choice, if humanity and life on Earth is to flourish and grow.

I urge you to help restore our planet in every way you can. What actions will you take?

SECTION IV
THRIVING BY MOVING EVER FORWARD

*"If you can't fly then run,
if you can't run then walk,
if you can't walk then crawl,
but whatever you do you have
to keep moving forward."*

Martin Luther King Jr.

Thriving by Moving Ever Forward

13 - Evolving—Aging with Soul

- Changing Ourselves and Making Transitions
- Process Steps for Evolving
- Courage, Humility, and Taking Care of Ourselves

14 - Gaining Wisdom

- Dimensions of Wisdom
- Shifts of Mind and Habits
- Lessons and Advice
- Writing an Ethical Will

13

EVOLVING—AGING WITH SOUL

"There is nothing noble in being superior to your fellow man. True nobility is being superior to your former self."

Ernest Hemingway

C hanging ourselves and making significant transitions in life are central aspects of evolving. Thriving implies that we are evolving. It might even require it. A portion of evolving can come naturally over time and by having many life experiences. However, much of our evolving comes from a conscious process involving serious self-examination and then working hard on what we discover—from our shortcomings and mistakes and from the pain we have felt or inflicted. It comes from accepting criticism. The truth is that we learn more from criticism than from praise. And while we don't wish suffering on ourselves or others, it is how we grow. We cannot evolve as much as we otherwise could without courage, risk taking, and humility. This is where our relationship with ourselves becomes critical,

along with support from people who matter to us. To evolve successfully, we need to love life and trust it cautiously.

Evolving with soul, which is related to but is different from
aging well (as discussed in chapter 2), is essentially about becoming
more of a human being and seeing human potential realized in us
individually. It includes developing a greater felt awareness of being
part of humanity. This involves having a sense of community with
all beings—human and nonhuman, alive and dead. Doing so gives
us a more complete picture of what life is all about. Evolving is
about becoming a more robust and better person by being more
compassionate, being a better listener, expanding our perspective,
and becoming more patient, encouraging, and loving. These are all
aspects of thriving.

We pay an enormous price if we don't do the work of evolving
and nurturing our true selves—our souls. We might forgo becoming
wiser. As Tryon Edwards said, "He that never changes his opinions,
never corrects his mistakes, will never be wiser on the morrow than
he is today." If we don't evolve, we can feel hollow, and we might
try to fill that void with useless additions and empty behaviors. A
sense of purposelessness and depression can set in, and in some cases,
anger.

Consciously evolving to become a better person is a distinct goal
and a part of my life purpose. For me, this process continues and is
far from complete.

Changing Ourselves and Making Transitions

*"When I was young, I admired clever people. Now that I am
old, I admire kind people."* Abraham Joshua Heschel

We encounter endings with some regularity in life, requiring us to make transitions and change ourselves. Sometimes change is forced upon us; other times, we choose to change. In both cases, change can be challenging. It involves many emotions and requires us to make choices and be committed to seeing it through. As Charles Glassman said, "There is only one way to survive and thrive when faced with circumstances that are out of our control and when we are unprepared: ADAPT." Indeed, by changing our thoughts, outlook, and habits, we can change—ourselves, and the world.

When we're navigating through changes and transitions, many emotions well up in us. As explained by William Bridges in his Transition Model,[103] transitions can initially lead to a whole set of emotions, including denial, anxiety, shock, fear, anger, and frustration. At some point, we enter into an exploration phase, which can involve different emotions like confusion, stress, skepticism, impatience, and approach-avoidance. Hopefully, new beginnings will arrive before long. These, too, can usher in a new set of emotions, such as being enthusiastic, energetic, and hopeful. At this point, we can be more creative and accepting. Coping successfully and navigating through all these emotions takes a lot of hard work and commitment.

As you navigate forward, ask, "What emotions am I feeling? What commitment is required?"

Over many years, I have worked hard to change things about myself that weren't working out well, thereby evolving as a person. I now am less judgmental, have more empathy, and am less inclined to jump in reflexively to solve a problem. I am a better listener, more able to listen to feelings, not just thoughts and ideas. This evolution, which includes giving up control (over most things), letting go of judgment (at least mostly), and giving up attachments, has been of significant value to me, emotionally and spiritually. It's made me happier and a better person. And I am now more drawn to wiser and more present people, maybe because they, too, have learned from their suffering.

Reviewing my own evolution, I also see that my goals have shifted. Since high school, I have had clear goals, and I still do, but now I feel far less of a need for achievement and a need to prove myself. Over time, I have shifted more of my focus to concern for others and the natural world, as well as to my own peace of mind, health, and happiness. At the same time, having a life of purpose and meaning remains vitally important to me.

In what ways are you evolving?

A few years ago, I wrote the following about evolving through six fundamental transitions:

1. **Income statement—Balance sheet**

   Not only in strictly financial terms, this is also about shifting from consuming to investing (again, not just financially); to being conscious of wasting, using natural and social resources wisely, borrowing, renting, and reusing rather than buying and discarding. The shift is from being only self-focused and independent to being focused on our planet and interdependent.

2. **Thinking—Feeling and the integration of the two**

   This involves recognizing that our rational, logical, problem-solving, thinking selves often take us only so far, and we never have all the information we need to make decisions. It reflects that our emotional, feeling self is valid and central to our existence. Often, how we feel about something is far more critical than what we think about it.

3. Doing—Being

In our complex and fast-paced world, it is essential to remember that motion is not progress. Being busy may mean missing out on the most important things. This shift underscores the importance of focusing on the important but non-urgent things rather than on the urgent, not-important things (the squeaky wheels surrounding our lives). Rather than focusing on doing, being can be about *how* we live, about quality of life, relationships, and everyday interactions.

4. Career—Calling

A career, even if deemed successful, does not necessarily mean that our best selves showed up or that we deeply cared for the work at hand. A calling does suggest these. A calling likely incorporates our passion and, at the same time, gives us joy, maybe deep joy and meaning. It might not lead to getting paid, at least financially. A calling might also include how we show up in our daily lives or how we treat people around us, including absolute strangers.

5. Struggle—Acceptance

Each shift from struggle to acceptance may be based on different factors requiring us to take a hard look at what is holding us back, where we are stuck, and what it takes to move forward. Reaching a place of acceptance may require a different way of holding the issue, a different perspective. Underlying acceptance is a willingness to change, grow, and be more empathetic and compassionate. This shift requires courage, determination, and humility.

6. **Résumé virtues—Eulogy virtues**

   What it takes to be successful in the workplace or to be seen as powerful or influential (call these external factors) is often quite different from those inner qualities that define a person's character—things like being kind, brave, honest, loyal, faithful, generous, caring, compassionate, and capable of deep love. These inner qualities may not lead to power, influence, or financial success.

Which of these transitions have you made or are you making?

We all make transitions as we go through our life cycles. With this in mind, I developed the transition exercises outlined below. Doing our homework as we're engaged in our life transitions can produce great results and make our transitions faster, smoother, and better overall. I recommend—especially as you begin your adult life and career, as well as at midlife and midcareer, maybe in your 40s (but really at any time!)—considering the following transition homework and creating the following three documents:

1. A rigorous and honestly written assessment of your professional and interpersonal talents, skills, likes, and dislikes. Ask yourself: What is special or unique about me? In what environment do I best contribute? What wisdom have I accumulated along the way?

2. A concentrated effort to discover or rediscover what you are passionate about. By looking beyond your personal/family and financial matters, ask yourself: What do I really care about? In which issues do I want to be involved?

3. A retirement plan based on your personal/family balance sheet and annual projected budget. Doing this long before you are seriously thinking of retiring can help enormously. There are many online retirement tools available without charge. Ask yourself: Am I financially independent now? If not, what amount of money do I need (lump sum or annually) to become financially independent? Very likely, such a written retirement plan will give you power by clarifying a wide variety of spending and lifestyle choices and giving you a sense of freedom and direction.

Of the three, the second piece of homework—clarifying one's passion—may be the most difficult for many people. This is also discussed in chapters 8 and 11. In this way, it might help to understand the difference between what you are paid to do for a living and your calling, as discussed above. One or a combination of these may help you clarify your passion: **Focus your attention on all aspects of life**, not just the old limited paradigm of work versus family. Consider a whole life portfolio, including career, financial, physical, emotional, and spiritual life, along with your relationships (with yourself, your life partner, family, friends, and others). Another way to clarify your passion is by serving others by **volunteering**. This can be in your local community (schools, youth sports teams, service projects, and the like) or by serving on a nonprofit board or committee. In addition, I recommend developing or updating a **statement of your life purpose**, which can also help you change and evolve. As Darryl Petersen wrote, "The way to having a truly vibrant and fulfilling later life is by finding a positive, developmental vision." He described this as incorporating a mission-driven goal based on our deepest interests, core values, greatest unique aptitudes and talents, and highest motivational patterns.[104] Writing a vision statement is also discussed in chapter 8 as a way to clarify one's purpose and meaning.

To assist you in this deep introspective process, committing to unplugging—taking one day off each week from shopping, media, and news—can be enormously beneficial, helping to recharge your battery regularly and provide much-needed perspective. Even more impactful would be to get away from your daily routine for an extended period, as discussed in chapter 2.

Which of these have you done, or will you do? By when will you commit to finishing all three pieces of transition homework?

Process Steps for Evolving

"Turn your wounds into wisdom." Oprah Winfrey

What does it take to change ourselves and evolve? It's easy to wonder where to begin. It's easier than we think to get lost and remain stuck. It's easy to look for love and other essential life ingredients in all the wrong places. And as Nikki Giovanni (or possibly Thomas Fuller) wrote, "Nothing is easy to the unwilling." It all starts with ourselves. This entails discovering what leads us to open and close to life's opportunities. It involves determining what things enable, empower, motivate, and allow us to be ready to march forward.

Think about something about yourself or your situation that you want to change. Are you ready? What steps do you need to take to get ready?

There is an architecture involved—a number of practical process steps—that can help us change and transition and evolve through life. It starts by knowing ourselves, sorting out our feelings and desires, and assessing our strengths, weaknesses, talents, and preferences. It includes understanding the people and events that have contributed to what's going on and evaluating what went well, what didn't, and what we did that contributed, both good and bad. This requires honesty and mental toughness. Writing down your thoughts about these issues will often help clarify complex things.

At this stage, our personal qualities and outlook come into play. This involves many things, including:

Believing in ourselves, being positive, and being as optimistic as we can be

Being motivated and committed to ourselves and the desired outcome

Being prepared to shift our minds and being willing to create new habits

Being focused and not distracted

Having grit, resilience, and the courage to swim against the tide or to face power and disapproval

Being humble so we can admit to mistakes and listen to others' advice and opinions

Being prepared and having the necessary energy and stamina to make progress and stay the course

Tapping into our accumulated wisdom

Committing to our ongoing evolution as a caring and compassionate person with gratitude and humility

We also need to determine whether we can change by ourselves or if we need to check in with someone else, maybe a partner. We may need to discuss the situation with a good friend to get further clarity or to enlist support. If the issue is deep, we might need to seek professional or spiritual help.

And it's essential to understand what might be holding us back and blocking us. Then we can sort out what we can do to get unblocked. At first, just notice what the voices in your head are saying. Sometimes what blocks us comes from deep-seated cultural things we've grown up with or voices from parents or other key people in our lives. Often, they arise from habitual and damaging processes and habits, like sabotaging ourselves.

There's no secret formula or magic recipe; however, a few things might help you make changes and evolve. Here are a few techniques:

- Using appreciative inquiry[105] to explore your past successes and accomplishments
- Uncovering and challenging limiting beliefs
- Shifting your perspective and reframing your perceptions
- Clarifying and aligning with your values
- Connecting with your passion and purpose in life
- Imagining new future possibilities, with yourself as a dreamer, realist, and critic
- Tapping into your nonverbal experiences
- Creating new self-talk
- Building more resourceful states and enlarging your network of relationships with people who can be of assistance and support

Which of these have you used? Which were particularly useful?

Creating options we wish for ourselves is essential. David Brower[106] told the following story: A man is sitting in a rowboat on a large lake. Suddenly, the boat begins to leak. The man tries to bail out the water, but it's coming in faster than he can bail. The man looks to the closest shore, which is far away. He is afraid to try to swim all the way. So, he stays in the rowboat, which is sinking. He stays there waiting and hoping for a raft to come along.

Instead of just waiting and hoping for something to change, as the story above describes, there are many times when we need to be mentally tough so that we can create options for ourselves. We also need to be honest with ourselves—injecting necessary humility—about our need to evolve with a new approach, attitude, or outlook.

Think about a specific difficult personal problem. What will it take for you to make a change or evolve? What "raft" can you construct so you can leave the boat?

Once we have designed some options, making a decision can be complex. Maybe we're not ready to choose among our options. There are many times when things are not so clear, simple, or straightforward. Our situation remains confusing, or even if we know what's going on, we don't have a plan or the courage to implement one. If this is the case for you, it might help to look and see what steps can be taken, even if baby steps initially, to get ready to change and try something new.

It might come down to being willing to take a risk. Taking a risk with something new might require summoning courage, because what you want to try might not work out, and you might worry that it will impact you or others in ways you can't foresee. And, frankly, even after all this, you still might need more time—perhaps you're simply not yet ready to change. Be patient, keep working on becoming ready, and don't give up.

But sometimes, we're paralyzed with fear. Remember that many fears are only imagined. Push down hard to avoid letting your fears be bigger than your dreams. At these times, you have to reach deep, love yourself, get needed support, and summon your courage and commitment to yourself to find the keys to harnessing your power of choice.

From there, you can create a plan. Sometimes the plan needs to be more than a feel-good vitamin and needs to be a severe-pain reliever. Often, it might help to talk to friends to get feedback about your plan, to help you find clarity. Reading or listening to information from psychologists, philosophers, experts, and religious leaders about a specific issue may also help you develop a plan. Be sure your plan identifies things you need, and then be sure to ask for them. If other people don't know what we need or want, it isn't surprising when they don't provide us with those things.

You'll need to revise your plan as you obtain more information and feedback. Some things might work, and others won't. As Publilius Syrus said in Rome 2000 years ago, "It's a bad plan that can't be changed." In addition, your plan will likely involve some experimenting and require you to try new things, some of which might be uncomfortable. You must embrace the risks involved, including the risk that your plan may meet with disapproval or failure. When that happens, it's encouraging to remember that change and experimenting with new, hopefully better, approaches are a central part of life. Your plan and action steps might need to change several times. So have grit, and be persistent. Continue to commit and invest.

A considerable amount is involved in carrying out such a plan beyond these steps above. So much of our success in implementing a plan involves managing ourselves and our outlook on others. This includes seeing the best in ourselves and others. Give others the benefit of the doubt. It's best to pace ourselves, taking time to absorb the myriad feelings and events swirling around. We need to be patient with ourselves and others. And be willing to be surprised, even in small steps and things. We must understand that our reality is incomplete and may not be accurate. There will be times when we must face some hard realities and accept the truth we have long ignored. There are times when we need to let go. There are times when we will need to forgive ourselves or others. There are times when we need to move on. And throughout, we need to be kind and gentle with ourselves and others.

Changing and evolving might also require us to let go of critical things holding us back and making us anxious. Frequently, this includes letting go of the overwhelming and burdensome influences of our parents (or other key formative people) and getting any of those negative voices out of our heads. For some people, this happens earlier in life, but for others, this might happen in their 60s and 70s, or maybe never. To move on and let those voices go, we need to find our own voice to discover who we are and what we value.

What are the negative influences holding you back? What influences (good and bad) are your parents continuing to have on you?

And here's another thing. To help us evolve along our journey, we can be open to moments when we let go and make an almost instantaneous change of attitude or habits—what I might call "miracles." These might range from highly emotional things to even simple and mundane ones, like flossing or getting daily exercise. Those moments are when a person who has been psychologically stuck in the dark for a long time metaphorically gets out of their chair, goes over to the light switch, and turns it on, deciding to finally make a significant change or to let go of something important. Getting out of our chairs and turning on the light takes only a few seconds. Suddenly letting go and getting unstuck is an exhilarating type of evolving.

My own most recent miracle happened when I let go of a strong, well-rationalized view that venting my feelings and frustrations was a good thing. I had rationalized that venting was akin to pressure being released by tectonic plates shifting. That this would lessen the chance of a huge earthquake later. I had held on to this view for decades. It had not worked, and in fact, tended to solidify my hurt or bad feelings by putting words to them. It harmed people hearing me talk about this under the guise of venting. One day, I stopped venting entirely. I'm delighted!

What "miracles" have you had? Where are you stuck? What "miracles" would you like to experience?

Another juicy process step I highly recommend considering for changing and evolving into a whole person is this: *living your legacy while you are still alive.* Living a legacy while we are alive is a way to age well and evolve, providing a source of joy and fulfillment. This is so important that it is also discussed in chapter 8 on purpose and meaning and in chapter 14 about gaining wisdom. While we are alive and living vigorously, we can let our true selves be seen and appreciated, which is central to being authentic. Our legacy doesn't have to be a bolstering of our ego but rather an expression of generosity and desire for heartfelt connection. We can live our life fully, accepting its challenges and opportunities. As we contemplate the future, our hearts can open wide, and we can consider the world that has not yet appeared. These are spiritual actions based on hope and kindness, which can extend the range and depth of our relationships far into the future and make us bigger people, people who are thriving.

What legacy are you creating?

Courage, Humility, and Taking Care of Ourselves

"Life shrinks or expands in proportion to one's courage." Anaïs Nin

Evolving—aging with soul—requires that we successfully navigate the many passages that life presents to us.[107] This involves making active decisions and often necessitates that we have the courage to take some uncomfortable risks. As Thomas Moore explains in *Ageless Soul: The Lifelong Journey toward Meaning and Joy*, if we closely observe the workings of life, we can realize that we have two choices available to us—life or death. By embracing the life principle, we move forward and accept the invitations life presents to us for more fulfillment, greater vitality, and the possibility of thriving. Alternatively, we can opt for the death principle, choosing to remain in our comfort zone, avoiding new ideas and experiences. Along our journey, it might be helpful to remember Winston Churchill's words "Success is not final; failure is not fatal; it is the courage to continue that counts." And along with our courage, it is also essential to believe in ourselves, knowing that our mistakes and failed experiments don't define us.

With this in mind, we can honor anyone of any age who has said yes to life and becomes a person who commits to evolving into wholeness. Being whole involves utilizing our heart, soul, mind, strength, and ability to see our flaws. We can also feel honor for ourselves, knowing when we have tried and sometimes failed, and knowing when we have risen above our comfort level to affirm the opportunities life has presented. This is a central aspect of thriving.

Think about a change you are considering. What decisions are involved? What will be uncomfortable? What will require courage?

In addition to courage, changing and evolving requires humility. When we are humble, we understand that we don't have all the answers. When we have humility, we know we can be wrong, and we understand that a change we're thinking of making might not be successful. In these ways, having humility can be of significant help by opening us up to more options and allowing us to listen to opinions that differ from ours.

To change and evolve, in what ways will you need to be humble?

Let's face it, changing, transitioning, and evolving often involve many steps and can be difficult. Of course, it's important to focus on our desired destination, being sure to include critical aspects—for example, taking ethics, impacts on the environment, or people and their feelings into account. But we also need to focus on the journey and take care of ourselves as we make progress along the way. To help focus on the journey, we should be kind and appropriately patient with ourselves. We can celebrate the small wins all along the way.

Don't wait until the end to celebrate. The end might not be what you thought it would be. Be open to surprises.

It helps to take a long view of time. Slowing things down will allow us to appreciate our own beauty, which can keep us vital. It can also replenish our sense of ourselves and the world. It helps to seek stillness, solitude, and silence, where it's much easier for us to sort things out. Going out into nature might be of great help. At such times, we become able to breathe life into ourselves and into others as well.

14

GAINING WISDOM

"Be wise not only in words but in deeds; mere knowledge is not the goal but action."

The Talmud

Life throws both the good and the bad at us, and we can become wise in the process as we reflect on life and our experiences. What is wisdom? What does it mean for a person to be wise? Wisdom covers an enormous number of things we face in life. Wisdom is not about how old we are, as, indeed, some young people have "old souls." But wisdom generally comes about as a cumulative process of living life. Thriving goes hand in hand with gaining wisdom.

This chapter caps off the previous 13 chapters, each encompassing elements of wisdom and helpful advice. This chapter, specifically about wisdom, has to start with a critical caveat: these thoughts I have collected from others and with a few additions of my own are only a work in progress. Becoming wise is never-ending. The following are a number of aspects I particularly appreciate. I hope you will too.

Dimensions of Wisdom

"A smart person knows what to say. A wise person knows whether to say it or not." David Wolfe

Let's start by investigating wisdom and the characteristics of a wise person. Wisdom is only one type of intelligence. According to John Levy, what we ordinarily characterize as intelligence seems to constitute three quite different qualities—intellectual power, knowledge, and wisdom—which we tend to confuse and lump together.[108] We can be strong in one and weak in another.

The first type of intelligence is intellectual power and mental acuity. This is the typical definition of intelligence and is what intelligence tests aim to evaluate. However, there are many forms of mental ability, of which IQ assesses only the more academic one. Other forms of intelligence include the mental agility of a fine athlete, aesthetic sensibility, talents for understanding and dealing with people (emotional intelligence quotient, or EQ), and something called "street smarts." These are all forms of mental ability, though they're often undervalued or overlooked, partly because they're difficult to measure. Intelligence appears to be largely determined by genetics, but regardless of our innate abilities, we can develop our mental powers through discipline, training, effort, study, and guidance.

Knowledge is the second quality that we include under intelligence. We acquire knowledge as we become more self-aware and gain understanding of others, as we gain expertise in a specific field, and as we understand more about the world around us. We use our cognitive abilities to acquire knowledge, but having knowledge does not mean the same as having a high level of intellectual capacity. One example is that we've all encountered people with exceptional mental gifts but who have limited knowledge or understanding.

The third quality of being intelligent is having wisdom, which doesn't necessarily accompany the other two aspects of intelligence. Wisdom is what it takes to make good choices in life—to recognize options, distinguish among them, and select and follow those that will be most creative and rewarding. This is probably the most generally recognized characteristic of wise people: they make good decisions. When we thrive, we make good decisions. Here are several main aspects of wisdom:[109]

- Wise people value and work at self-understanding and acceptance. We gain a deeper understanding of our motivations, worries, and biases—all in order to discover our true selves.

- Being wise means being conscious of and accepting of our limitations. This includes realizing that there is a fixed amount of time in a day, that we need to refuel and recharge periodically, and that our lives are not eternal.

- Becoming wiser involves setting priorities for our choices and our lives, abandoning paths that do not lead to significant benefits. It means saying no to other options.

- Growing in wisdom means becoming increasingly willing and able to accept responsibility for our own lives. Blaming others for our setbacks and failures becomes uninteresting and irrelevant.

- The wise person has the patience and vision to forgo immediate pleasure and endure discomfort in pursuit of goals of long-term value.

- Making wise choices frequently entails breaking away from "either/or" thinking when making decisions, and identifying and exploring other options.

- Wise people recognize and trust what their intuition tells them without downplaying or minimizing the importance of their conceptual abilities.

- Wisdom has a broad viewpoint and considers the bigger picture, enabling wise people to view situations and issues from a rational, emotional, and practical perspective.

- Wisdom means growing beyond self-centeredness and recognizing the importance of our interdependence—with those close to us, with people globally, and with all life.

- Wise people understand that a focus on competitiveness and self-promotion hinders us from reaching our fullest potential.

- Wise people become increasingly unconcerned about how they are judged. This is greatly liberating, allowing us to pursue more enduringly fulfilling objectives.

- Humor is often an attribute that characterizes wise people. Wisdom brings an ability to treat one's misfortunes and failings with some amusement, moving beyond self-absorption.

- Wisdom is accompanied by humility, enabling us to be accepting of who we are and not feel the need to present a false image to others or ourselves.

- Wise people lead a life guided by spiritual beliefs and values. This involves exploring the deeper meaning and purpose of life and embracing a sense of a higher reality beyond the material and mundane world.

- Wisdom encompasses love, recognizing that love gives life its meaning and vitality. As Jack Kornfield wrote in *Buddha's Little Instruction Book*, "In the end these things matter most: How well did you love? How fully did you live? How deeply did you learn to let go?"[110]

Take time to review each of these. Which of these aspects of wisdom do you have? Which would you like to have? How do you plan to obtain them?

Life teaches us, in all sorts of ways, that becoming wiser is our most valuable and desirable goal and the one most worthy of our efforts. As Krista Tippett writes, "Wisdom can and does emerge precisely through those moments when we have to hold seemingly opposite realities in a creative tension and interplay: power and frailty; birth and death; pain and hope; beauty and brokenness; mystery and conviction; calm and buoyancy; mine and yours."[111]

And wisdom can come about as we naturally age and have more experiences in life, as we understand ourselves and the world more and remain dedicated to being lifelong learners. Gaining wisdom often comes when we learn from our mistakes. We gain wisdom from our suffering and as we recognize the suffering we have caused in others. Sometimes we gain wisdom as we become bored or dissatisfied with other goals. And sometimes, our wisdom can happen because we find guidance from a coach, a wise mentor, or a spiritual teacher, whether alive or not.

Shifts of Mind and Habits

"The only person who can transform your life is the one you see every day in the mirror. Be the one who shapes your own destiny."
Federico Navarrete

Everyday wisdom involves how we face and deal with the experiences of our lives and how we react to the unexpected and often complicated aspects of life. Krista Tippett believes we can allow our wisdom to patiently change us from the inside with gentle shifts of mind and habits. These ongoing shifts reflect a state of thriving and include the following:

Being curious, wondering, and questioning allows us to see wisdom in the world or feel it in ourselves. Being curious about why we are here and finding delight in the vastness of reality of life is a gift. Wondering and planting questions in the many parts of life helps us see and touch and helps us heal.

Having humility is not about getting small, not about debasing ourselves, but about approaching everything and everyone else with a readiness to see goodness and be surprised. Humility means recognizing that we are never really running the show, never really in control. This allows for a lightness of step, not a heaviness of heart.

Engaging in generous listening involves letting go of assumptions, being willing to be surprised, and taking in ambiguity. Generous listening yields better questions that reveal something unknown and invite honesty and dignity. Generous listening is powered by curiosity.

Using words well allows complex thoughts and deep feelings to be revealed so we can effectively engage others. We rely on words to tell the truth about the world and ourselves. Simplifications, like slogans, while sometimes clever, often miss the mark. We know that words of feeling matter, since facts alone don't tell us the whole story.

Appreciating beauty gives us fresh eyes for seeing and even fully becoming our best selves. This is more than just niceness and loveliness. Appreciating beauty is a great opportunity to allow light into the process of becoming a more substantial being.

Recognizing our body includes knowing that our physical selves carry trauma and joy and our capacity for responding to life and one another. It means knowing that life is never perfect but fluid and constantly evolving. It shows us that life is, by definition, messy and always leaning toward disorder and surprise. Our bodies tell us that we are as much about softness as fortitude in any moment and that we're always in need of care and tenderness. The body is where every virtue lives or dies.

Choosing hope is a cognitive, behavioral process, not an emotion. It is what we have when relationships are trustworthy and people have faith in our abilities, and it is what we learn when we experience adversity. Hope is a function of struggle. Critical thinking without hope is cynicism. But hope without critical thinking is naïveté. As distinct from idealism or optimism, hope is a choice. Like every virtue, it can become a habit, which then becomes spiritual muscle memory. Hope has the power to shift the world on its axis.[112]

Which of these habits resonate most with you? In which ways are you cultivating your wisdom?

Lessons and Advice

"You just can't let life happen to you, you have to make life happen." Idowu Koyenikan

Sometimes we gain wisdom by observing and sometimes by engaging with others. Here are 10 questions to ask yourself as well as important people in your life, including your life partner:

1. What are some of the most important lessons you have learned in your life?

2. What kind of advice would you have about getting or staying married?

3. What advice do you have about raising children?

4. What advice can you share about finding fulfilling work and how to succeed in a career?

5. Difficult or stressful experiences can yield important lessons. Is that true for you? Can you give me examples of what you have learned?

6. Do you see any turning points—key events or experiences—that changed the course of your life?

7. What would you say you now know about living a happy and successful life that you didn't know when you were 20?

8. What would you say are the primary values or principles that you live by?

9. Have you learned any lessons regarding staying in good health?

10. What advice would you give people about growing older?

How would you answer these questions? Who else will you ask these questions?

While there are many books and lists about secrets to success, here's one from *Investor's Business Daily* I especially like called "10 Secrets to Success":

1. How you think is everything. Always be positive. Think success, not failure. Beware of a negative environment.

2. Decide upon your true dreams and goals. Write down your specific goals and develop a plan for reaching them.

3. Take action. Goals are nothing without action. Don't be afraid to get started now. Just do it.

4. Never stop learning. Go back to school or read books. Get training and acquire skills.

5. Be persistent and work hard. Success is a marathon, not a sprint. Never give up.

6. Learn to analyze details. Get all the facts and all the input. Learn from your mistakes.

7. Focus your time and money. Don't let other people or things distract you.

8. Don't be afraid to innovate; be different. Following the herd is a sure way to mediocrity.

9. Deal and communicate with people effectively. No person is an island. Learn to understand and motivate others.

10. Be honest and dependable; take responsibility. Otherwise, numbers 1 through 9 won't matter.[113]

Which of these are you following? What are the highest priorities for you to work on?

Here are a few additional thoughts of my own about wisdom:

- "Perfect" can genuinely be the enemy of "good." It's common to hear people say they want something to be perfect—weddings and relationships are two examples. This is messy and can lead to disappointment or not making an important decision. Nothing is perfect. Instead, focus on excellence. It's okay to have high standards, but be flexible.

- Our wedding should be a cornerstone of our lives, not a capstone.

- During any significant event—a wedding (ours, or a friend's or family member's), a big vacation, a retirement party, and the like—there could easily be some things that don't go as planned—the flowers, the food, a costume malfunction, a speech, whatever. Just know that you can make these glitches a part of the humorous retelling and make it okay.
- Don't assume. Remember, when we assume, we are making an ASS out of U and ME. It's better to ask questions or get clarification.
- It's much harder to edit what's not there than what is already written.
- Listen. Ask questions. Be patient.
- Live authentically. Be true to yourself. Take the time to sort out who you are and what you stand for.
- Be kind. Be kind to yourself. Be kind to everyone else. Animals too!

What aspects of wisdom would you like to add?

There are many things written about wisdom and living life well. I especially appreciate these:

All I Really Need to Know I Learned in Kindergarten, by Robert Fulghum

https://www.goodreads.com/work/quotes/2399046-all-i-really-need-to-know-i-learned-in-kindergarten

Here are a few of my favorites from Fulghum: "Share everything." "Say you're sorry when you hurt somebody." "Live a balanced life—learn some and think some and paint and sing and dance and work some every day."

What I Wish I Knew When I Was 20, by Tina Seelig

https://www.elise.com/blog/tina_seelig_what_i_wish_knew_when_i_was_20

My favorites of Seelig's are: "Every problem is an opportunity for a creative solution." "Try lots of things and keep what works."

"The 25 Principles for Adult Behavior," by John Perry Barlow

https://www.mickeyhart.net/news/the-25-principles-for-adult-behavior-by-john-perry-barlow-25395

My favorites of Barlow's 25 are: "Be patient no matter what." "Don't badmouth: assign responsibility, not blame." "Say nothing of another you wouldn't say to them." "Concern yourself with what is right rather than who is right." "Love yourself." "Endure."

There is much wisdom contained in these works. I encourage you to read them slowly and return to them often. Incorporating them into your life may help you thrive.

And then there's maybe my all-time favorite, Desiderata, which is framed and hung in our house, where I see it every day.

Desiderata

GO PLACIDLY amid the noise and the haste, and remember what peace there may be in silence. As far as possible, without surrender, be on good terms with all persons.

Speak your truth quietly and clearly; and listen to others, even to the dull and the ignorant; they too have their story.

Avoid loud and aggressive persons; they are vexatious to the spirit.

If you compare yourself with others, you may become vain or bitter, for always there will be greater and lesser persons than yourself.

Enjoy your achievements as well as your plans. Keep interested in your own career, however humble; it is a real possession in the changing fortunes of time.

Exercise caution in your business affairs, for the world is full of trickery. But let this not blind you to what virtue there is; many persons strive for high ideals, and everywhere life is full of heroism.

Be yourself. Especially do not feign affection. Neither be cynical about love; for in the face of all aridity and disenchantment, it is as perennial as the grass.

Take kindly the counsel of the years, gracefully surrendering the things of youth.

Nurture strength of spirit to shield you in sudden misfortune. But do not distress yourself with dark imaginings. Many fears are born of fatigue and loneliness.

Beyond a wholesome discipline, be gentle with yourself. You are a child of the universe no less than the trees and the stars; you have a right to be here.

And whether or not it is clear to you, no doubt the universe is unfolding as it should. Therefore be at peace with God, whatever you conceive Him to be. And whatever your labors and aspirations, in the noisy confusion of life, keep peace in your soul. With all its sham, drudgery and broken dreams, it is still a beautiful world. Be cheerful. Strive to be happy.

By Max Ehrmann © 1927

Writing an Ethical Will

"I want what I love to continue to live; and you whom I love and sang above everything else to continue to flourish, full-flowered."
Pablo Neruda

An ethical will is a window into the soul of the writer. It can be as simple as a letter to our loved ones expressing our thoughts and feelings about our life and hopes and blessings for our survivors' future. The purpose of an ethical will is to articulate and convey to our loved ones key things, including the beliefs, values, and family, spiritual, and religious traditions that we hold dear; what we want most for and from our loved ones; and the wisdom we have acquired during our lifetime. A good book on this subject is *Ethical Wills: Putting Your Values on Paper*, by Barry Baines, MD.

In the late 1990s, I came across the concept of an ethical will. I immediately began reading and learning about this concept and its importance. In 1999, I wrote my first ethical will, and I have updated it periodically since then. Among many things, it includes encouraging my loved ones to work hard, play hard, and work before play. It also suggests that in a world full of people who couldn't care less, they try to be someone who cares more.

Preparing an ethical will for those who live on after we die is a blessing. And remember, as Charles Spurgeon wrote, "A good character is the best tombstone. Those who loved you and were helped by you will remember you . . . Carve your name on hearts, not marble." I encourage you to create an ethical will of your own.

Why create an ethical will? There are many personal reasons for writing an ethical will. Maybe foremost is a wise saying, "Words that come from the heart enter the heart." Our heritage of values, experience, and personal connection is, to many, so much more important than the family's legacy of material possessions. Yet the concept of an ethical will is not well known, and even if known, how many of us will put as much time, effort, and thought into these matters as we do into our material will and legacy? Many of the reasons to write an ethical will reflect the power we have now and the impact we can have well into the future. Here is a partial list of reasons to write an ethical will:

- When we write an ethical will, we learn a lot about ourselves.
- It helps us identify what we value most and what we stand for.
- By articulating what we value now, we can take steps to ensure the continuation of those values for future generations.
- We all want to be remembered, and we all will leave something behind.
- If we don't tell our stories and the stories from which we come, no one else will, and they will be lost forever.
- It helps us come to terms with our mortality by creating something of meaning that will live on after we are physically gone.
- It provides a sense of completion in our lives.

An ethical will has no formal structure or required elements. However, here are suggestions for several aspects you might address:

- Opening—Consider: To whom do you wish to write? Why are you writing this? Example: "I write this to you, my children and grandchildren, in order to . . ."
- My Family/Our Family—Consider who is who (your parents, siblings, antecedents); geographical identity; the world from

which you came; family stories and events that helped shape your family.

- My Life/My Personal History—Consider people who strongly influenced your life; important early influencers, memories, and events that helped shape your life; how you feel looking back over your life and what sense you make of it (successes, regrets, choices made, what you've learned).

- My Beliefs, Values, and Practices—Ethical ideals and practices; spiritual and religious insights and observances.

- Personal Connections—Gifts of favorite possessions (particular item to a specific person, along with a story about the item); forgiveness ("I forgive you for _____. I would like to ask your forgiveness for _____.").

- Closing/Blessings—"I want you to know how much I love you and how grateful I am to you. My ardent wishes for you are _____."

- Memorial Service and Funeral Arrangements—Do you have any specific requests? Example: "Please request that in lieu of flowers, donations be sent to _____."

- Additional Considerations—How to convey the ethical will (read aloud, audio, or video); when to convey the ethical will (upon your death, at a child's 18th birthday, at a major life event, etc.); technical considerations—where the ethical will is to be kept; how it is referred to in your material will; how often it's revised).[114]

Here are some people who might consider writing an ethical will:

- Couples upon engagement—for sharing a common set of values

- Expectant and new parents—to provide a framework for child-rearing

- Growing families—for teaching values to their children
- People middle-aged and beyond—for converting life experience into wisdom and passing this on to future generations
- Those at the end of life or going through a big health scare—to add to the transcendent dimension of life. If you do write an ethical will, you will leave a gift to the future, and the not-yet-born children of your children's children will thank you and bless you for it.

It's also important to consider when to give your ethical will to your loved ones. Here are a few questions to think about: Are they old enough? Or should it be placed in safekeeping for them until they reach a certain age or maturity? Do you want to give your ethical will to your loved ones while you are still alive and able to discuss it with them? Most important, if you have any unfinished personal relationship business, *now* is the time to resolve it and make peace.

In my case, I decided to give my ethical will to my wife and children only recently, and at the same time, I gave them a draft of this book. I plan to put a copy of my ethical will in safekeeping for my grandchildren until they're older.

When will you write your ethical will? When will you give it to your loved ones?

TAKING HOLD OF THE REINS!

"Whatever you can do or dream you can, begin it.
Boldness has genius, power, and magic in it.
Begin it now."

Goethe

We began this journey together at my business school reunion with the realization that in life, we are constantly dealt cards that we proceed to play. However, unlike in a card game, we do have some control over which cards we receive. And we certainly have an enormous amount to do with how we play them by making choices along the way. When we sit down to play, are we focused? Do we have the energy and stamina to play well? Do we even sit down at the table? We have more power to choose and to create the possibility of thriving than we might know.

As discussed in the 14 chapters of this book, by making choices in nearly every aspect of our lives, we can create opportunities in order to thrive in ways we know and in ways we have not yet even begun to appreciate. Living vigorously, flourishing, and prospering means that we are thriving in all dimensions—personally, professionally, with friends, partners, and family, out in the world, and actively engaged in our precious world as we move forward in life. Maybe not equally at all times, but certainly in some integrated combination. And likely with a slightly different emphasis at different stages of our lives—for example, organizational leadership and management are likely more important in terms of thriving in the middle of our lives. Some aspects of thriving are constants—having character and being grateful, for example. What it takes to thrive varies to some degree for each of us. And remember that thriving is an average state over time—it's the climate, not today's weather.

Our Power to Choose Is All around Us

"Creativity that carves out the future
Performance that measures up time after time
Relationships that nurture and empower
Effectiveness that triumphs over circumstances." Werner Erhard

It's more possible than we know to build an integrated life and run on all cylinders. We have the power to make choices that determine who we are, to decide how we feel and how we react. We can do the hard work to engage mindfully, to know ourselves, to speak up and be heard, to grow, to take responsibility, and to take action. We have the power to develop good habits and character, to be positive, and to make a positive difference all around us. We can advocate for ourselves—with partners, friends, and bosses. And we can listen and then listen harder. We can always learn—from our experiences and from others. We can learn from our mistakes and from things that didn't go well. We can be lifelong learners. We can do the same thing repeatedly but see it differently, like seeing a movie another time. Or we can have new experiences altogether, even if that means summoning up our courage and humility to get out of our comfort zone. We can gain wisdom, which will help us make good and conscious decisions. We can grow and evolve into better human beings. We can learn to let go. During the course of our lives with many endings, including our final one, we can finish strong. Strong and flexible like a willow branch.

We can be financially literate and prudent. We can determine how much money and how many material possessions are enough for ourselves and our families. And, far more than material and financial success, we can be a person living a life of purpose and meaning, full of positive emotions and outlook, with a deep relationship with ourselves and others. Like packing a suitcase for a trip—it starts with an empty bag, and then we decide what to put in it. We can also determine what to take out of it and what to let go of. We can have a life of "coulds" rather than a life of "shoulds"; we can have a life of choice. We can talk to ourselves instead of listening to ourselves: instead of listening to our complaints, fears, and doubts, we can talk to ourselves with words of truth and encouragement. And, as Henry Ford said, "Whether you think you can, or you think you can't—you're right."

We don't have to be our own worst enemy. We don't have to shoot ourselves in the foot. We can also stop undermining ourselves with bad mental habits that work against our best interests. Through careful and honest assessment, these mental saboteurs can be sorted out, diminished, and more than offset by developing our sage selves.

The lyrics from the Eagles' song "Take It Easy" come to mind: *"Don't let the sound of your own wheels drive you crazy."* Instead, we can strive to have confidence, believe in ourselves, and trust our intuition and gut instincts. We can seek out and listen closely to advice and be supportable and coachable.

We can be prepared emotionally, intellectually, and physically. We can set our expectations appropriately. We can realize that we're better off in many cases by not having expectations and simply enjoying what happens. We can be responsible and successful people while recognizing that much of life is out of our control and that there is a healthy dose of luck involved in our lives. We can find humor in things, and we can laugh at ourselves. We can heal ourselves. We can be forgiving, grateful, generous, and kind. To ourselves. To everyone else. To animals and Mother Earth. I offer for consideration the Ojibway Indian Prayer:

> *Grandfather, Sacred One,*
> *Teach us love, compassion, and honor,*
> *That we may heal the earth*
> *And heal each other.*

This powerful perspective opens a sense of possibility. It's not about healing the world by making a huge difference. It's about healing the world that touches us personally. We need to constantly remind ourselves that our world is abundant with beauty, courage, and grace. We need to be willing to be guided by love, compassion, and forgiveness.

We can combine power with love to engage with nearly every aspect of the world we live in. Martin Luther King Jr. suggested that power—the ability to achieve purpose—without love is dangerous and oppressive, while love without power is weak and ineffective. He eloquently said, "The concepts of love and power have usually been contrasted as opposites—polar opposites—so that love is identified with the resignation of power, and power with the denial of love." He went on to say, "It is this collision of immoral power with powerless morality which constitutes the major crisis of our time."

We can live our own lives. We can swim against the tide of culture and society or even our family. We can stop living on autopilot. We have the power to make choices, take action, choose whom to listen to, invent new things—habits, rituals, and traditions. As Steve Jobs[115] said in his commencement speech at Stanford University in June 2005, "Your time is limited, so don't waste it living someone else's life. Don't be trapped by dogma—which is living with the results of other people's thinking. Don't let the noise of others' opinions drown out your own inner voice. And most important, have the courage to follow your heart and intuition. . . . Stay Hungry. Stay Foolish."

We can define success our own way and not rely on someone else's definition. Our success can include having integrity and being authentic. We don't have to chase success. Instead, if we decide to make a difference, success will find us. And remember that there is no such thing as overnight success. Love the process, and you'll love what the process produces. Next time you "fail," remember that it's not meant to define you. It's meant to refine you. Each day we can focus on what we get to do, not what we have to do. Remember that life is a gift, not an obligation.

What We Practice, We Become

"After a long time of practice, our work will become natural, skillful, swift, and steady." Bruce Lee

In our world of interdependence with strangers from afar, and at this time of urgent environmental challenges, we must realize the magnitude of the stakes for which we are playing. Our challenges, at times, seem overwhelming. Choices we make individually and collectively could lead to a world we don't want to—or worse, can't—live in. But it doesn't have to be that way. Instead, making good choices in order to thrive might be precisely what we need to address the real work at hand. As Franklin D. Roosevelt said in the dark days of 1938, just before the beginning of World War II, "We observe a world of great opportunities disguised as insoluble problems." We have the power, the critically important power, to transform an obstacle into an opportunity.

We have the power to transform the environment around us. As Jon Gordon asks, "When placed in boiling water, do you want to be an egg or a carrot or a coffee bean? An egg hardens, a carrot weakens, but a coffee bean transforms the water into something more."[116] We can look for opportunities within our families and with friends, neighbors, and others to love, be charitable and philanthropic, care, and serve. We don't have to be great to serve, but we have to serve to be great.

We can unleash the enormous and often hidden power in our own lives in what we do and how we affect the world. We can rise above circumstances. We can create in our own lives and the world the possibility of wholeness and meaning that goes well beyond only progress, that reflects hope beyond mere pragmatism, that leads to being love, not only feeling love. As Krista Tippett writes, "We are born with the capacity to find the hidden light in all events and all people, to lift it up and make it visible once again and thereby to restore the innate wholeness of the world. . . . this is, of course, a collective task. . . . We are all healers of the world."[117]

We have the power to make choices and thrive, but only if we are willing to think, see ourselves and the situation clearly, take responsibility for ourselves, and take action. As Marshall McLuhan wrote, "There is no inevitability as long as there is a willingness to contemplate what is happening." Only then, when we are ready, motivated to change and move forward, can we engage our power to choose which course of action to take.

It all comes down to this: *to be the author of our own story*, we have to take hold of the reins, we have to be in the driver's seat and steer, and we have to set sail. President Franklin D. Roosevelt made this point quite well when he wrote, "To reach a port we must set sail— sail, not tie at anchor; sail, not drift." This takes work and practice. What we practice, we become. In Krista Tippett's words, "We only learn to walk when we risk falling down, and this equation holds— with commensurately more complex dynamics—our whole lives long."[118] We must keep practicing and continue to have the humility and courage to take risks and grow so that our power to make choices will be available to us. Otherwise, other people will take control and make choices for us. The options that could have been available to us will no longer be available. It all starts with ourselves. We can make good choices that allow us to live vigorously, flourish, prosper, and thrive.

Enjoy the ride. Smile and laugh more. We have only one ride through life. So please make the most of it.

I hope you, dear reader, feel the encouragement and love I am sending your way. I truly hope this book and the questions and exercises in it have been or will be valuable to you as you continue your journey!

"This is the true joy in life, the being used for a purpose recognized by yourself as a mighty one; the being a force of nature instead of a feverish, selfish little clod of ailments and grievances complaining that the world will not devote itself to making you happy. . . . I want to be thoroughly used up when I die, for the harder I work the more I live. I rejoice in life for its own sake. Life is no 'brief candle' to me. It is a sort of splendid torch, which I have got hold of for the moment; and I want to make it burn as brightly as possible before handing it on to future generations."

George Bernard Shaw, *Man and Superman*

"Could this coming year be the best year of your life thus far? What would it take for this to be so?"

Randolph M. Selig

ENDNOTES

Section I: Thriving Personally

Chapter 1: Building Character

1. Based on Jon Gordon, "Twenty Ways to Get Mentally Tough," excerpt from *Training Camp: What the Best Do Better Than Everyone Else* (John Wiley and Sons, 2009), 77.

2. Based on Jon Gordon, "10 Ways to Succeed with Zero Talent." https://jongordon.com/positivetip/zerotalent.html.

3. Adverse childhood experiences (ACEs) are specific experiences by those under age 18 that can lead to toxic stress and trauma. https://www.joiningforcesforchildren.org/what-are-aces/. Take the ACE quiz: https://www.npr.org/sections/health-shots/2015/03/02/387007941/take-the-ace-quiz-and-learn-what-it-does-and-doesnt-mean. An ACE score is a tally of different types of abuse, neglect, and other hallmarks of a rough childhood. Taking the test, I scored a 3. In addition, as an adult, I developed chronic eye problems. Because of this, I became grateful for modern medicine and excellent doctors and medical care. I also gained humility.

4. Rushworth Kidder, *Shared Values for a Troubled World: Conversations with Men and Women of Conscience* (Jossey-Bass,

1994), chapter 8. Kidder was president of the Institute for Global Ethics.

Chapter 2: Relationship with Ourselves

5. Saul McLeod, "Erik Erikson's 8 Stages of Psychosocial Development," SimplyPsychology, May 3, 2018, https://www.simplypsychology.org/Erik-Erikson.html. Eric Erikson (1902–1994) was a German-American developmental psychologist and psychoanalyst known for his theory on the psychological development of human beings. He may be most famous for coining the phrase *identity crisis*.

6. Barbara Larrivee, "Building Up Your Defenses against Stress," presented at the 2nd Educating Mindfully Conference, Itasca, IL, February 2020. Larrivee is an educator, researcher, author, and workshop leader. She wrote *A Daily Dose of Mindful Moments: Applying the Science of Mindfulness and Happiness*.

7. From the Quadrinity Model created by Bob Hoffman. https://www.hoffmaninstitute.org/the-process/.

8. Shirzad Chamine, *Positive Intelligence: Why Only 20% of Teams and Individuals Achieve Their True Potential and How You Can Achieve Yours* (Greenleaf Book Group, 2012), 19, 20. www.positiveintelligence.com.

9. The 10 saboteurs referred to in *Positive Intelligence* are the Judge, the master saboteur we all have, and nine accomplices—the Controller, Stickler, Avoider, Hyper-Achiever, Pleaser, Victim, Restless, Hyper-Vigilant, and Hyper-Rational. These nine reflect a person's style (assert, earn, or avoid) and motivation (independence, acceptance, or security).

10. Thomas Moore, *Ageless Soul: The Lifelong Journey toward*

Meaning and Joy (St. Martin's, 2017), 195. Moore is an American psychotherapist, former monk, and writer of popular spiritual books, including the *New York Times* bestseller *Care of the Soul*. He writes and lectures in the fields of archetypal psychology, mythology, and imagination. The writings of Carl Jung and James Hillman influenced his work.

11. Moore, *Ageless Soul*, 21.
12. Ram Dass, born Richard Alpert in 1931, was an American spiritual teacher, psychologist, guru of modern yoga, and author of 13 books. His 1971 book *Be Here Now* helped popularize Eastern spirituality and yoga in the West.
13. Moore, *Ageless Soul*, 6.
14. Daniel Levitin, *Successful Aging: A Neuroscientist Explores the Power and Potential of Our Lives* (Dutton, 2020), 118.
15. Moore, *Ageless Soul*, 8.

Chapter 3: Managing Ourselves

16. Stephen Covey, *The 7 Habits of Highly Effective People: Powerful Lessons in Personal Change* (Simon & Schuster, 2020), 73, 109, 167.
17. Paul Johnson, "The Rhino Principle," *Forbes*, January 30, 2006. https://www.Forbes.com/forbes/2006/0130/031.html. Johnson is an eminent British historian and author.

Chapter 4: Money

18. John Levy, unpublished article "How Much Money Is Enough?" 1993. John was a personal friend and an advisor to families about financial matters. He is the author of *Inherited Wealth: Opportunities and Dilemmas*.

19. Randolph M. Selig, unpublished article "The Use and Abuse of Money in Community," 1996.

Chapter 5: Emotions

20. Chip Conley, *Emotional Equations: Simple Truths for Creating Happiness + Success* (Free Press, 2012), 87, 110, 123, 188, 196.

21. Notes from a lecture by Fred Luskin, PhD, on "The Science of Happiness," April 17, 2019. Luskin is the director of the Stanford University Forgiveness Projects, a senior consultant in health promotion at Stanford University, and a professor at the Institute for Transpersonal Psychology, as well as an affiliate faculty member of the Greater Good Science Center. He is the author of *Forgive for Good: A Proven Prescription for Health and Happiness.*

22. Maslow's hierarchy of needs is a theory of motivation that states that five categories of human needs dictate an individual's behavior. Those needs, from lowest to highest, are physiological, safety, love and belonging, esteem, and self-actualization.

23. Carl Jung (1875–1961) was a Swiss psychiatrist and psychoanalyst who founded analytical psychology. Among the central concepts of analytical psychology is individuation—the lifelong psychological process of differentiating the self from each individual's conscious and unconscious elements. Jung considered this to be the main task of human development. For more on Jung's views on happiness and suffering, go to www.jungiancenter.org.

24. Jonathan Clements, "The Pursuit of Happiness: Six Experts Tell What They've Done to Achieve It," *Wall Street Journal,* December 6, 2006. https://www.wsj.com/articles/SB116536 873558741857.

25. Ram Dass and Mirabai Bush, *Walking Each Other Home: Conversations on Loving and Dying* (Sounds True, 2018), 47, 80.

26. Krista Tippett, *Becoming Wise: An Inquiry into the Mystery and Art of Living* (Penguin Random House, 2016), 104. Krista Tippett is an American journalist, author, and entrepreneur. She created and hosts the public radio program and podcast *On Being*. https://onbeing.org/series/podcast/. In 2014, Tippett was awarded the National Humanities Medal for "thoughtfully delving into the mysteries of human existence."

27. Tippett, *Becoming Wise*, 9.

28. Gary Chapman, *The 5 Love Languages: The Secret to Love That Lasts* (Northfield, 2015).

29. John Gottman, "John Gottman on Trust and Betrayal," Greater Good Magazine, October 29, 2011. https://greatergood. berkeley.edu/article/item/john_gottman_on_trust_and_ betrayal. Gottman is an American psychological researcher and clinician who has written more than a dozen books about relationships, marriage, and families.

30. Brené Brown, "The Power of Vulnerability," TED Talk, 2010. https://www.ted.com/talks/brene_brown_the_power_of_vulnerability?language=en.

31. This parody of the 12 Steps program is unattributed. https://thehaynesclinic.com/12-step-programme/ the-twelve-step-to-insanity/.

32. Patrick Lencioni, *Getting Naked: A Business Fable about Shedding the Three Fears That Sabotage Client Loyalty* (Jossey-Bass, 2010). See book summary at https://medium.com/@/leenasn/ book-summary-getting-naked-a-business-fable-about-shedding-the-three-fears-that-sabotage-client-632d2bbc295f.

While this book speaks about consultants, clients, and business, much of this applies to relationships of all types, including with family, friends, and work colleagues.

33. Dass and Bush, *Walking*, 47, 80.

34. Dass and Bush, *Walking*, 131.

35. Dass and Bush, *Walking*, 62, 70.

36. Dass and Bush, *Walking*, 116.

37. Stephen Levine, *A Year to Live: How to Live This Year As If It Were Your Last* (Bell Tower, 1997), 40.

38. Aldous Huxley (1894–1963) was an English writer and philosopher. He wrote nearly 50 books—both novels and nonfiction works—as well as wide-ranging essays, narratives, and poems. His best-known book is *Brave New World*.

39. Steve Jobs (1955–2011) was an American business magnate, industrial designer, investor, and media proprietor. He was the chairman, chief executive officer, and cofounder of Apple Inc., the Pixar chairman and majority shareholder, and the founder, chairman, and CEO of NeXT. Jobs is widely recognized as a pioneer of the personal computer revolution of the 1970s and 1980s, along with Apple cofounder Steve Wozniak. Jobs posthumously received the Presidential Medal of Freedom in 2022.

40. Stephen Levine and Ondrea Levine, *Who Dies? An Investigation of Conscious Living and Conscious Dying* (Anchor Books, 1982), 73, 74.

41. Levine and Levine, *Who Dies?* 74, 75.

42. Levine and Levine, *Who Dies?* 75.

43. First published in 1984 by Saskia Davis. Since then, many versions have been written. See symptomsofinnerpeace.net.

Chapter 6: Spirituality and Religion

44. Abraham Joshua Heschel (1907–1972) was an American rabbi and one of the leading Jewish theologians and Jewish philosophers of the 20th century. He was internationally known as a scholar, author, and activist. His social consciousness led him to participate actively in the civil rights movement. He wrote a dozen books, including *Man Is Not Alone: A Philosophy of Religion.*

45. Martin Buber (1878–1965) was a prolific author, scholar, literary translator, and political activist whose writings ranged from Jewish mysticism to social philosophy, biblical studies, philosophical anthropology, education, politics, and art. He wrote *I and Thou* (originally *Ich und Du*) (Martino, 2010), first published in 1923 in German and first translated to English by Ronald Gregor Smith in 1937. The quote from Buber is nicely explained at monkstownparish.ie/reflection/god-is-found-in-relationships.

46. Thomas Moore, *A Religion of One's Own: A Guide to Creating a Personal Spirituality in a Secular World* (Penguin, 2015), chapter 1.

47. Moore, *A Religion of Own's Own,* 7.

48. Moore, *A Religion of One's Own,* 8.

49. Moore, *A Religion of One's Own,* 12.

50. Ron Wolfson, *The Spirituality of Welcoming: How to Transform Your Congregation into a Sacred Community* (Jewish Lights, 2006).

51. Lawrence Hoffman, *ReThinking Synagogues: A New Vocabulary for Congregational Life* (Jewish Lights, 2006).

52. Wolfson, *The Spirituality of Welcoming,* 8, 145.

53. Wolfson, *The Spirituality of Welcoming,* 11, 15, 52, 55–60.

54. Hoffman, *ReThinking Synagogues*, 61, 89, 172.

55. Wolfson, *The Spirituality of Welcoming*, 15, 143.

56. Wolfson, *The Spirituality of Welcoming*, 121–122.

57. Hoffman, *ReThinking Synagogues*, 142.

58. Hoffman, *ReThinking Synagogues*, 141.

59. Wolfson, *The Spirituality of Welcoming*, 23, 111.

60. Wolfson, *The Spirituality of Welcoming*, 183.

61. Hoffman, *ReThinking Synagogues*, 159.

62. Hoffman, *ReThinking Synagogues*, 168.

63. Hoffman, *ReThinking Synagogues*, 103, 139.

Chapter 7: Gratitude

64. Arthur C. Brooks, "Choose to Be Grateful. It Will Make You Happier," *New York Times*, November 21, 2015. https://www.nytimes.com/2015/11/22/opinion/sunday/choose-to-be-grateful-it-will-make-you-happier.html.

65. Jon Gordon, "The Power of Thank You." https://jongordon.com/positive-tip-power-of-thank-you.html.

66. Robert Heilbroner, *The Great Ascent: The Struggle for Economic Development in Our Time* (New York: Harper & Row, 1963), 33–36.

67. Jeremy Adam Smith, "6 Habits of Highly Grateful People," Daily Good, March 19, 2014. http://www.dailygood.org/story/663/6-habits-of-highly-grateful-people-jeremy-adam-smith.

68. Adapted from a poem by Ruth F. Brin (1921–2009). Brin was a literary pioneer famous for her poetry, prayer services, scholarly articles, and children's books.

Chapter 8: Purpose and Meaning

69. From a handout given to me by Darryl Petersen (1935–2006). Petersen was a career/life development counselor and coach with a personal mission to empower people to realize their full unique potential in their professional and personal lives. I worked with him before starting my own company. I will be eternally grateful for all his coaching.

70. Abraham Maslow (1908–1970) was an American psychologist who was best known for creating Maslow's hierarchy of needs, a theory of psychological health predicated on fulfilling innate human needs in priority, culminating in self-actualization. See https://positivepsychology.com/self-actualization/.

71. See jungutah.org/blog/individuation-and-the-unlived-life-of-the-parents.

72. Viktor Frankl, *Man's Search for Meaning* (Beacon, 2006), 145.

73. Jill Suttie and Jason Marsh, "Is a Happy Life Different from a Meaningful One?" Greater Good Magazine, February 25, 2014. https://greatergood.berkeley.edu/article/item/happy_life_different_from_meaningful_life.

74. See Eisenhower's use-of-time model: Team Asana, "The Eisenhower Matrix: How to Prioritize Your To-Do List," Asana.com, October 4, 2022. https://asana.com/resources/eisenhower-matrix.

Section II: Thriving Together

Chapter 9: Relationships with Others

75. Nathan Hill, *The Nix* (Penguin Random House, 2016), 127.

76. Howard Hunter was the 14th president of the Church of Jesus

Christ of Latter-Day Saints. He wrote this as a Christmas wish. See https://ldsquotations.com/author/howard-w-hunter/.

77. Thomas Moore, *Ageless Soul: The Lifelong Journey toward Meaning and Joy* (St. Martin's, 2017), 225.

78. John Gottman, *The Relationship Cure: A Five-Step Guide to Strengthening Your Marriage, Family, and Friendships* (Three Rivers, 2001), chapter 1.

79. Esther Wojcicki, *How to Raise Successful People: Simple Lessons to Help Your Child Become Self-Driven, Respectful, and Resilient* (Houghton Mifflin Harcourt, 2020), 7.

80. Carolyn R. Shaffer and Kristin Anundsen, *Creating Community Anywhere* (CCC Press, 2005), 41.

81. Shirzad Chamine, *Positive Intelligence: Why Only 20% of Teams and Individuals Achieve Their True Potential and How You Can Achieve Yours* (Greenleaf Book Group, 2012), 17–20.

82. Condoleezza Rice is an American diplomat and political scientist who is the current director of the Hoover Institution at Stanford University. She served as United States secretary of state from 2005 to 2009 and was the national security advisor from 2001 to 2005.

83. Daniel Yankelovich, *The Magic of Dialogue: Transforming Conflict into Cooperation* (Simon & Schuster, 1999), 36–46.

84. Samuel Osherson, *Finding Our Fathers: The Unfinished Business of Manhood* (Free Press, 1986). Osherson is a psychologist affiliated with the Harvard University Health Services.

85. Samuel Osherson, "Each Father Shapes the Life of a Son in a Different Way," *U.S. News & World Report*, June 16, 1986, 60, 61.

86. Robert Gilman, "Guidelines for Eco-Village Development: Eight Steps to Creating Your Own Sustainable Community,"

Living Together (IC#29), Context Institute, Summer 1991, 60. https://www.context.org/iclib/ic29/gilman2/.

Chapter 10: Leadership and Management

87. Simon Sinek, "How Great Leaders Inspire Action," TED Talk. https://www.ted.com/talks/simon_sinek_how_great_leaders_inspire_action?language=en.

88. Warren Bennis, *On Becoming a Leader* (Perseus, 1989), 202. Bennis (1925–2014) was a pioneer in leadership studies and a scholar who advised presidents and business executives on how to become successful leaders. *On Becoming a Leader* is his seminal work, exemplifying Bennis's core belief that leaders are not born—they are made.

89. Rich Karlgaard, "Four Styles of Leadership," *Forbes*, October 15, 2009. https://www.forbes.com/forbes/2009/1102/opinions-rich-karlgaard-digital-rules.html?sh=3ae5adef5dc7.

90. Burke Miller is an author, executive coach, and leadership educator. For the past 25 years he has been helping people become more potent and inspiring in their professional lives. Miller has continued to develop his thinking about the four continuums and now refers to them as inspiration, integrity, clarity, and courage. He wrote about these in *A Sacred Trust: The Four Disciplines of Conscious Leadership* (Earth Connection, 2019). See www.burkemiller.com.

91. The four habits summarized here were taken from notes I took at a presentation by Stephen Covey in 1995.

92. Stephen Covey, *The 7 Habits of Highly Effective People: Powerful Lessons in Personal Change* (Simon & Schuster, 2020), 235, 273, 307.

Section III: Thriving in the World

Chapter 11: Charity, Philanthropy, and Service

93. Os Guinness, *Long Journey Home: A Guide to Your Search for the Meaning of Life* (Waterbrook Press, 2001).

94. Jim Morgan, "A Humble Approach to Giving," Applied Wisdom for the Nonprofit Sector, November 21, 2021. https://www.appliedwisdomfornonprofits.org/a-humble-approach-to-giving/. Morgan, who for nearly three decades led the high-tech powerhouse Applied Materials Inc. both to financial success and to designation as one of America's most admired companies and best places to work, is a philanthropist and has written several books, including *Applied Wisdom* and *Applied Wisdom for Non-Profits*.

95. Marge Piercy, "To Be of Use," *Circles on the Water* (Alfred A. Knopf, 1982). Piercy has written 17 novels and 20 volumes of poetry. You can listen to her read her poem "To Be of Use" by going to her website, www.margepiercy.com.

96. Richard Chait, William Ryan, and Barbara Taylor, *Governance as Leadership: Reframing the Work of Nonprofit Boards* (John Wiley & Sons, 2005).

97. Krista Tippett, *Becoming Wise: An Inquiry into the Mystery and Art of Living* (Penguin, 2017), 34.

Chapter 12: Conservation and the Environment

98. Henry David Thoreau (1817–1862) was an American naturalist, essayist, poet, and philosopher. He is best known for his book *Walden*, a reflection upon simple living in natural

surroundings, and his essay "Civil Disobedience," an argument for disobedience to an unjust state. Among Thoreau's lasting contributions are his writings on natural history and philosophy, in which he anticipated the methods and findings of ecology and environmental history, two sources of modern-day environmentalism.

99. Donella Hager "Dana" Meadows (1941–2001) was an American environmental scientist, educator, and writer. She is best known as the lead author of the books *The Limits to Growth* and *Thinking in Systems: A Primer.*

100. Aldo Leopold, *A Sand County Almanac: And Sketches Here and There* (Oxford University Press, 1949).

101. Robert Muller (1923–2010) was an international civil servant with the United Nations. Serving with the UN for 40 years and rising to assistant secretary-general, he wrote about his ideas concerning world government, world peace, and spirituality. He was known by some as "the philosopher of the United Nations." He was named Laureate of the UNESCO Prize 1989 for Peace Education.

102. Andres Edwards, *The Sustainability Revolution: Portrait of a Paradigm Shift* (New Society, 2005), 21–23.

Section IV: Thriving by Moving Ever Forward

Chapter 13: Evolving—Aging with Soul

103. William Bridges is an organizational consultant who found that guiding people through transition was the key to successful change. He identified three stages of transition, and his model strives to help understand the feelings people experience through a change process. See https://wmbridges.com/about/what-is-transition/.

104. This is from a handout Petersen gave me when we worked together.

105. Appreciative Inquiry is a strengths-based positive approach to personal, leadership, and organizational change. Juliette Tocino-Smith, "How to Apply Appreciative Inquiry: A Visual Guide," Positive Psychology, May 21, 2019. https://positivepsychology.com/appreciative-inquiry-process/.

106. David Brower (1912–2000) was a prominent environmentalist and the founder of many environmental organizations, including the John Muir Institute for Environmental Studies, Friends of the Earth (1969), Earth Island Institute (1982), North Cascades Conservation Council, and Fate of the Earth Conferences. From 1952 to 1969, he served as the first executive director of the Sierra Club and served on its board three times.

107. Thomas Moore, *Ageless Soul: The Lifelong Journey toward Meaning and Joy* (St. Martin's, 2017), 53.

Chapter 14: Gaining Wisdom

108. John Levy, excerpts from an unpublished 1995 article entitled "Wisdom and Wealth." John was a personal friend and an advisor to families about financial matters. He is the author of *Inherited Wealth: Opportunities and Dilemmas*.

109. Levy, "Wisdom and Wealth."

110. Jack Kornfield, *Buddha's Little Instruction Book* (Bantam, 1994), 85.

111. Krista Tippett, *Becoming Wise: An Inquiry into the Mystery and Art of Living* (Penguin, 2017), 266.

112. Tippett, *Becoming Wise*, 9–11.

113. Erin Falconer, "10 Secrets to Success," blog, January 17, 2008. https://pickthebrain.com/blog/10-secrets-to-success/ Originally printed in *Investor's Business Daily*, March 30, 2003.

114. From an interfaith workshop I led in December 1998.

Taking Hold of the Reins!

115. " 'You've Got to Find What You Love,' Jobs Says," Stanford News, June 12, 2005. https://news.stanford.edu/2005/06/12/youve-got-find-love-jobs-says/.

116. Jon Gordon and Damon West, *The Coffee Bean: A Simple Lesson to Create Positive Change* (John Wiley and Sons, 2019). See https://jongordon.com/books/coffeebean/

117. Krista Tippett, *Becoming Wise: An Inquiry into the Mystery and Art of Living* (Penguin, 2017), 25.

118. Tippett, *Becoming Wise*, 13.

RECOMMENDED BOOKS BY CHAPTER

Author's Note: The descriptions of the books have been edited by me but come primarily from Amazon book reviews. Several of these recommended books are referred to in multiple chapters.

Chapter 1: Building Character

Quiet: The Power of Introverts in a World That Can't Stop Talking, Susan Cain

In *Quiet*, Cain argues that we dramatically undervalue *introverts* and shows how much we lose in doing so. She charts the rise of the *"Extrovert* Ideal" throughout the 20th century and explores how deeply it has come to permeate our culture.

The Energy Bus: 10 Rules to Fuel Your Life, Work, and Team with Positive Energy, Jon Gordon

The Energy Bus takes readers on an enlightening and inspiring ride that reveals *10* secrets for approaching *life* and *work* with *positive* and forward thinking that leads to true accomplishment at *work* and at home.

Originals: How Non-Conformists Move the World, Adam Grant

In *Originals*, Grant addresses the challenge of improving the *world* from the perspective of becoming *original*: choosing to champion novel ideas and values that go against the grain, battle conformity, and buck outdated traditions. How can we originate new ideas, policies, and practices without risking it all?

It's Better Than It Looks: Reasons for Optimism in an Age of Fear, Gregg Easterbrook

This book looks at current conditions compared to the past and concludes that life is much better now than in the past. It's better in almost every way— we live longer, are more affluent, are less subject to violence, and are more democratic. Along the way, Easterbrook acknowledges that there are plenty of problems to overcome and threats to avoid. He argues that the fixes are available, though nothing in life is simple.

Chapter 2: Relationship with Ourselves

Positive Intelligence: Why Only 20% of Teams and Individuals Achieve Their True Potential and How You Can Achieve Yours, Shirzad Chamine

Chamine reveals how to achieve one's true potential for both professional success and personal fulfillment. His groundbreaking research exposes 10 well-disguised mental "Saboteurs." Executives in his Stanford lectures conclude that these Saboteurs cause "significant harm" to achieving their full potential.

With *Positive Intelligence*, the secret to defeating these internal foes can be learned. *Note:* This book is also referred to in chapter 9.

The 7 Habits of Highly Effective People: Powerful Lessons in Personal Change, Stephen Covey

Covey sets forth a holistic, integrated, principle-centered approach to solving personal and professional problems. With penetrating insights and pointed anecdotes, he reveals a step-by-step pathway for living with fairness, integrity, service, and human dignity—principles that give us the security to adapt to change and the wisdom and power to take advantage of the opportunities that change creates. *Note:* This book is also referred to in chapters 3 and 10.

David and Goliath: Underdogs, Misfits, and the Art of Battling Giants, Malcolm Gladwell

Gladwell challenges our concepts of "advantage" and "disadvantage" and shows how players labeled "underdog" use that status to their advantage and prevail. He also shows how certain academic "advantages," such as getting into an Ivy League school, have downsides, in that being a "big fish in a small pond" at a less-prestigious school can lead to greater confidence and a better chance of success in later life. Gladwell also promotes the idea of a "desirable difficulty," such as dyslexia, a learning disability, that may force those who have it to develop better listening and creative problem-solving skills.

Good Morning, I Love You: Mindfulness and Self-Compassion Practices to Rewire Your Brain for Calm, Clarity, and Joy, Shauna Shapiro, PhD

Good Morning, I Love You brings alive the brain science behind why we feel the way we do—about ourselves, each other, and the world—and explains why we get stuck in thinking that doesn't serve us. We are hardwired to be self-critical and negative, and this negativity is constantly undermining our experience of life. In lively, short chapters laced with science, wisdom, and story, Shapiro, one of the leading scientists studying the effects of mindfulness on the brain, shows us that acting with kindness and compassion toward ourselves is the key.

Thrive: The Third Metric to Redefining Success and Creating a Life of Well-Being, Wisdom, and Wonder, Arianna Huffington

In *Thrive*, Huffington talks candidly about her own challenges with managing time and balancing business with family life. She makes an impassioned case for the need to go beyond the two traditional metrics of success—money and power—to redefine what it means to be successful in today's world. The third metric Huffington calls for includes our well-being, our ability to draw on our intuition and inner wisdom, our sense of wonder, and our capacity for compassion and giving. Drawing on the latest research and findings in the fields of psychology, sports, sleep, and physiology, *Thrive* illuminates the profound and transformative effects of meditation, mindfulness, unplugging, and giving.

Blink: The Power of Thinking without Thinking, Malcolm Gladwell

Blink is a book about how we think without thinking—about choices that seem to be made in an instant, in the blink of an eye, that aren't actually as simple as they seem. Why are some people brilliant decision-makers while others are consistently inept? Why do some people follow their instincts and win, while others end up stumbling into error? How do our brains really work—in the office, in the classroom, in the kitchen, and in the bedroom? And why are the best decisions often impossible to explain to others?

Books about Aging Well and Retirement

Successful Aging: A Neuroscientist Explores the Power and Potential of Our Lives, Daniel Levitin, PhD

Levitin looks at the science behind what we all can learn from those who age joyously, as well as how to adapt our culture to take full advantage of older people's wisdom and experience. Using research from developmental neuroscience and the psychology of individual differences, Levitin reveals resilience strategies and practical, cognitive-enhancing tricks everyone should use as they age.

Younger Next Year: Live Strong, Fit, Sexy, and Smart—Until You're 80 and Beyond, Chris Crowley and Henry Lodge, MD

Cowritten by one of the country's most prominent internists, Dr. Henry "Harry" Lodge, and his star patient, the 73-year-old Chris Crowley, this book shows us how to turn back our biological clocks—how to put off 70 percent of the usual problems of aging (weakness, sore joints, poor balance) and eliminate 50 percent of serious illness and injury. The key to the program is found in Harry's Rules: Exercise six days a week. Don't eat crap. Connect and commit to others. There are seven rules based on the latest findings in cell physiology, evolutionary biology, anthropology, and experimental psychology. Dr. Lodge explains how and why they work, and Crowley, who is living proof of their effectiveness, gives the just-as-essential motivation.

Ageless Soul: The Lifelong Journey toward Meaning and Joy, Thomas Moore

Moore teaches readers how to embrace the richness of experience and how to take life on, accept invitations to new vitality, and feel fulfilled as they get older. Moore reveals a fresh, uplifting, and inspiring path toward aging, one that need not be feared but instead embraced and cherished. In Moore's view, aging is the process of becoming a more distinctive, complex, fulfilled, loving, and connected person. He argues for a new vision of aging: as a dramatic series of initiations rather than a diminishing experience, one that each of us has the tools—experience, maturity, fulfillment—to live out. *Note:* This book is also referred to in chapters 9 and 13.

The Blue Zones: Lessons for Living Longer from the People Who've Lived the Longest, Dan Buettner

In *The Blue Zones*, longevity expert Dan Buettner has blended his lifestyle formula with the latest longevity research to inspire lasting behavioral change and add years to your life. Buettner draws from his research on extraordinarily long-lived communities—Blue Zones—around the globe to highlight their lifestyles, diets, outlooks, and stress-coping practices. A long, healthy life is no accident. It begins with good genes, but it also depends on good habits. If you adopt the proper lifestyle, experts say you may live up to a decade longer. The recipe for longevity, Buettner has found, is deeply intertwined with community, lifestyle, and spirituality.

Repacking Your Bags: Lighten Your Load for the Rest of Your Life, Richard Leider and David Shapiro

This book helps you repack your four critical "bags" (place, relationship, work, and purpose); identify your gifts, passions, and values; and plan your journey, no matter where you are in life. People everywhere feel overwhelmed today, weighed down by countless responsibilities and buffeted by never-ending changes in their personal and professional lives. *Repacking Your Bags* shows readers how to climb out from under these burdens and find the fulfillment that is missing in their lives. In this wise and practical guide, Leider and Shapiro help you weigh all that you're carrying, leverage what helps you live well, and let go of those burdens that merely weigh you down.

Refire! Don't Retire: Make the Rest of Your Life the Best of Your Life, Ken Blanchard and Morton Shaevitz

Refire! Don't Retire asks readers the all-important question: as you look at the years ahead, what can you do to make them satisfying and meaningful? Blanchard and Shaevitz point out that some people see their later years as a time to endure rather than an exciting opportunity. Both research and common sense confirm that people who embrace these years with energy and gusto— rather than withdrawing and waiting for things to happen—consistently make the rest of their lives the best of their lives. Readers will find humor, practical information, and profound wisdom in *Refire! Don't Retire*. Best of all, they will be inspired to make all the years ahead truly worth living.

How to Retire Happy, Wild, and Free: Retirement Wisdom That You Won't Get from Your Financial Advisor, Ernie Zelinski

How to Retire Happy, Wild, and Free helps readers create an active, satisfying, and happy retirement in such a way that they don't need a million dollars to retire. Zelinski explains that the key to achieving an active and satisfying retirement involves much more than having adequate financial resources; it also encompasses all other aspects of life—leisure activities, creative pursuits, physical well-being, mental well-being, and solid social support. What sets this retirement book apart from all the others is its holistic approach to the fears, hopes, and dreams people have about retirement.

Chapter 3: Managing Ourselves

Essentialism: The Disciplined Pursuit of Less, Greg McKeown

McKeown describes a disciplined, systematic approach for determining where our highest point of contribution lies, then making the execution of those things almost effortless. The way of the Essentialist is the path to being in control of our own choices. It is a path to new levels of success and meaning. McKeown makes a compelling case for achieving more by doing less. He reminds us that clarity of focus and the ability to say no are both within our grasp.

Outliers: The Story of Success, Malcolm Gladwell

Gladwell takes us on an intellectual journey through the world of "outliers"—the best and the brightest, the most famous and the most successful. He asks the question: what makes high-achievers different? His answer is that we pay too much attention to what successful people are like and too little attention to where they are from: that is, their culture, their family, their generation, and the idiosyncratic experiences of their upbringing.

The Tipping Point: How Little Things Can Make a Big Difference, Malcolm Gladwell

Gladwell brilliantly explores and illuminates the tipping-point phenomenon, which is changing how people worldwide think about selling products and disseminating ideas. The tipping point is that magic moment when an idea, trend, or social behavior crosses a threshold, tips, and spreads like wildfire. Just as a single sick person can start an epidemic of the flu, so too can a small but precisely targeted push cause a fashion trend, the popularity of a new product, or a drop in the crime rate.

Chapter 4: Money

Your Money or Your Life: 9 Steps to Transforming Your Relationship with Money and Achieving Financial Independence, Vicki Robin and Joe Dominguez

Robin and Dominguez offer a nine-step program for living a more meaningful life, showing readers how to get out of debt, save money, reorder financial priorities, resolve inner conflicts, save the planet, and convert problems into opportunities.

Inherited Wealth: Opportunities and Dilemmas, John Levy

Filled with wisdom and insights for families, inheritors, and their advisors, *Inherited Wealth* explores a broad range of issues that often arise through the transmission of wealth within a family—and then responds to these in a healing and transformative way. Whether you are leaving an inheritance, are receiving one, or are a professional working with a family, this book identifies the major challenges and provides guidance for working through them. Ultimately, this book is about living an enriched life—one that includes personal and spiritual growth, contribution, and legacy. *Note:* This book is also referred to in chapter 14.

Voluntary Simplicity: Toward a Way of Life That Is Outwardly Simple, Inwardly Rich, Duane Elgin

Voluntary Simplicity is not a book about living in poverty; it is a book about living with balance. Elgin illuminates the changes that an increasing number of Americans are making in their everyday lives, adjustments in day-to-day living that are an active, positive response to the complex dilemmas of our time. By embracing the tenets of voluntary simplicity—frugal consumption, ecological awareness, and personal growth—people can change their lives and, in the process, save our planet.

The Courage to Be Rich: Creating a Life of Material and Spiritual Abundance, Suze Orman

Orman explains what it means to turn toward your money and to turn some of your money toward others. Ultimately, it means taking the courageous steps necessary to attain material and spiritual wealth. Practical, spiritual, and above all, soundly financial, *The Courage to Be Rich* is a book for today's challenging times.

More Money Than God: Living a Rich Life without Losing Your Soul, Steven Leder

Leder uses his experience as a religious leader and spiritual counselor to tackle money issues: keeping money from being a focal point, differentiating wants and needs, living morally while seeking the comfort that money brings, and teaching children about values involving money.

Think, Act, and Invest Like Warren Buffett: The Winning Strategy to Help You Achieve Your Financial and Life Goals, Larry Swedroe

This book provides a solid, sensible investing approach based on Buffett's advice regarding investment strategies. Swedroe argues that simple is better, that adopting basic investing principles always increases an investor's chance of success, and that Buffett is an excellent model for such investing.

Charles Schwab's New Guide to Financial Independence: Practical Solutions for Busy People, Charles Schwab

Schwab distills his 40-plus years of accumulated wisdom and explains how to define and set investment goals; prepare an investment plan, put the plan into action, and update the plan regularly; plan for your children's education or your retirement; cope effectively with the ups and downs of the market; and make sure you'll have enough for a comfortable retirement.

Chapter 5: Emotions

Emotional Equations: Simple Truths for Creating Happiness and Success, Chip Conley

Using brilliantly simple logic that illuminates the universal truths in common emotional challenges, *Emotional Equations* offers a way to identify the elements in our lives that we can change, those we can't, and how to better understand our emotions so they can help us rather than hurt us.

Happier: Learn the Secrets to Daily Joy and Lasting Fulfillment, Tal Ben-Shahar

In *Happier,* Professor Ben-Shahar brings the ideas of the Ivory Tower to Main Street, distilling the lessons and exercises from his course into a trove of practical wisdom. Grounded in the Positive Psychology movement and based on years of researching the works of scientists, academics, and philosophers, *Happier* emphasizes the importance of pursuing a life of both pleasure and meaning. Lessons, exercises, and "Happiness Boosters" cover self-esteem, empathy, friendship, love, achievement, creativity, spirituality, and humor.

30 Lessons for Loving: Advice from the Wisest Americans on Love, Relationships, and Marriage, Karl Pillemer

Drawing on interviews with 700 long-married elders, Pillemer's *30 Lessons for Loving* delivers timeless wisdom from a wide range of voices on everything from choosing "the one" to dealing with in-laws, money, children, and sex.

Whether readers are searching for the right partner or working to keep the spark alive, *30 Lessons for Loving* illuminates the path to lifelong, fulfilling relationships.

Getting the Love You Want: A Guide for Couples, Harville Hendrix and Helen LaKelly Hunt

Hendrix and Hunt present the relationship skills that have already helped hundreds of thousands of couples replace confrontation and criticism with a healing process of mutual growth and support. This practical guide describes the revolutionary technique of Imago Relationship Therapy, which combines a number of disciplines—including the behavioral sciences, depth psychology, cognitive therapy, and Gestalt therapy, among others—to create a program to resolve conflict and renew communication and passion.

Forgive for Good: A Proven Prescription for Health and Happiness, Frederic Luskin

Based on scientific research, this groundbreaking study from the frontiers of psychology and medicine offers startling new insight into the healing powers and medical benefits of forgiveness. Through vivid examples, Dr. Luskin offers a proven nine-step forgiveness method that makes it possible to move beyond being a victim to a life of improved health and contentment.

Walking Each Other Home: Conversations on Loving and Dying, Ram Dass and Mirabai Bush

Walking Each Other Home was written to enlighten and engage readers on the spiritual opportunities within the dying process. Ram Dass and Mirabai Bush generously share intimate personal experiences and timeless practices, told with courage, humor, and heart, gently exploring every aspect of this journey. The book includes guidelines for being a "loving rock" for the dying, and how to grieve fully and authentically, transform a fear of death, leave a spiritual legacy, create a sacred space for dying, and much more.

A Year to Live: How to Live This Year As If It Were Your Last, Stephen Levine

Levine, author of the perennial bestseller *Who Dies?* teaches us how to live each moment, each hour, each day mindfully—as if it were all that was left. Most of us go to extraordinary lengths to ignore, laugh off, or deny the fact that we are going to die, but preparing for death is one of the most rational and rewarding acts of a lifetime. It is an exercise that allows us to deal with unfinished business and enter into a new and vibrant relationship with life. Levine provides us with a yearlong program of intensely practical strategies and powerful guided meditations to help with this work so that whenever the ultimate moment does arrive for each of us, we will not feel that it has come too soon.

Chapter 6: Spirituality and Religion

A Religion of One's Own: A Guide to Creating a Personal Spirituality in a Secular World, Thomas Moore

In *A Religion of One's Own*, best-selling author and former monk Thomas Moore explores the possibilities of creating a personal spiritual style, either inside or outside formal religion. He recounts the benefits of contemplative living that he learned during his 12 years as a monk but also the more original and imaginative spirituality that he later developed and embraced in his secular life. Moore shares stories of others who are creating their own path and weaves their experiences with the wisdom of philosophers, writers, and artists who have rejected materialism and infused their secular lives with transcendence.

Peace Is Every Step: The Path of Mindfulness in Everyday Life, Thich Nhat Hanh

The deceptively simple practices of *Peace Is Every Step* encourage readers to work for peace in the world as they continue to work on sustaining inner peace by turning the "mindless" into the mindful. In the rush of modern life, we tend to lose touch with the peace that is available in each moment.

The Spirituality of Welcoming: How to Transform Your Congregation into a Sacred Community, Ron Wolfson

Writing with humor, verve, and candor, Wolfson sets forth a renewed vision of synagogues as energetic sacred communities—and outlines how you can transform your congregation into an inviting center of vibrant relationships and personal spiritual rejuvenation. This is a practical guide for envisioning—and transforming—your congregation into one of welcoming, learning, and healing.

Chapter 8: Purpose and Meaning

Ten Stupid Things Men Do to Mess Up Their Lives, Dr. Laura Schlessinger

In 10 vital, compelling chapters, Dr. Laura speaks her mind on chivalry, independence, ambition, strength, sex, matrimony, husbanding, parenting, boyishness, and machismo.

Man's Search for Meaning, Viktor Frankl

Psychiatrist Viktor Frankl's memoir has riveted generations of readers with its lessons for spiritual survival. Between 1942 and 1945, Frankl survived four different labor camps, including Auschwitz, while his parents, brother, and pregnant wife perished. Based on his own experience and the experiences of others he treated later in his practice, Frankl argues that we cannot avoid suffering, but we can choose how to cope with it, find meaning in it, and move forward with renewed purpose. Frankl's theory holds that our primary drive in life is not pleasure, as Freud maintained, but the discovery and pursuit of what we personally find meaningful.

Designing Your Life: Build a Life That Works for You, Bill Burnett and Dave Evans

Whether you're 20, 40, 60, or older, Burnett and Evans use their expertise to help you work through what you want—and how to get it. Their simple method will teach you how to use basic design tools to create a life that will work for you. Using real-life stories and proven techniques like reframing, proto-typing, and mind-mapping, you will learn how to build your way forward, step by positive step, to a life that's better by a design of your own making.

Long Journey Home: A Guide to Your Search for the Meaning of Life, Os Guinness

This book is a fine distillation of wisdom applied to the "big questions" of life's meaning and purpose. Rich in stories and profoundly personal as well as practical, it explores the great philosophies of life. It charts the road toward meaning taken by countless thoughtful seekers over the centuries.

Living a Life That Matters, Harold Kushner

In this inspiring book, Kushner addresses our craving for knowing that our lives and choices mean something. We sometimes confuse power, wealth, and fame with true achievement. We need to think of ourselves as good people and are troubled when we compromise our integrity to be successful and important. Rabbi Kushner suggests that the path to a genuinely successful and significant life lies in friendship, family, acts of generosity, and self-sacrifice.

He describes how, in changing the life of even one person in a positive way, we make a difference in the world, give our lives meaning, and prove that we do, in fact, matter.

The New American Dream: Finding Lifestyle Freedom on the Road, K. Shawtree

After interviewing more than 25 couples from four different generations (Generation Z, Millennials, Generation X, and Baby Boomers), the author has distilled common strategies, lessons, and advice for creating a life of freedom on the open road. Here's what the book offers: stories from travelers of all ages (with their secrets to success); steps to identify your personal goals and expectations for life on the road; lessons on how to travel as a family, as a couple, or solo; strategies and solutions for financing your adventure; tips on managing your relationship; tools for managing your money; lessons on things to avoid and things you must do; and more.

The Reinvention of Work: A New Vision of Livelihood for Our Time, Matthew Fox

In *The Reinvention of Work*, Fox brings together the work of Eastern and Western mystics, ancient, medieval, and modern, to propose a new paradigm for how we work and what we do.

Chapter 9: Relationships with Others

The Relationship Cure: A Five-Step Guide to Strengthening Your Marriage, Family, and Friendships, John Gottman

In this book, Gottman, one of the country's foremost relationship experts, presents a powerful, simple five-step program, based on 20 years of innovative research, for greatly improving all the relationships in your life—with spouses and lovers, children, siblings, and even colleagues at work. Packed with fascinating questionnaires and exercises developed in his therapy, *The Relationship Cure* offers a simple but profound program that will fundamentally transform the quality of all the relationships in your life.

How to Raise Successful People: Simple Lessons for Radical Results, Esther Wojcicki

The legendary teacher and mother shares her tried and tested methods for raising happy, healthy, successful children using TRICK: trust, respect, independence, collaboration, and kindness. Wojcicki's methods are the opposite of helicopter parenting. *How to Raise Successful People* offers essential lessons for raising, educating, and managing people to their highest potential. Change your parenting, change the world.

Finding Our Fathers: The Unfinished Business of Manhood, Samuel Osherson

A seminal classic, *Finding Our Fathers* examines the hidden struggle faced by millions of men: how to reconcile their childhood images of their fathers as silent, stoic breadwinners with the life they want to live now—embracing two-career marriages, closer ties with their children, and greater emotional awareness. Osherson shows you how your "unfinished business" with your father affects your relationships with your spouse, children, friends, and bosses—and how it can lead to a profound sense of loneliness, vulnerability, and rage. Osherson shows how you can resolve the inner conflict of the father-son relationship and begin to develop a new sense of strength and purpose in your family life and career.

Difficult Conversations: How to Discuss What Matters Most, Douglas Stone, Bruce Patton, and Sheila Heen

We attempt or avoid difficult conversations every day—whether dealing with an underperforming employee, disagreeing with a spouse, or negotiating with a client. *Difficult Conversations* provides a step-by-step approach to having those tough conversations with less stress and more success. You'll learn how to decipher the underlying structure of every difficult conversation; start a conversation without defensiveness; listen for the meaning of what is not said; stay balanced in the face of attacks and accusations; and move from emotion to productive problem-solving.

You Just Don't Understand: Women and Men in Conversation, Deborah Tannen

You Just Don't Understand is the book that brought gender differences in ways of speaking to the forefront of public awareness. With a rare combination of scientific insight and delightful, humorous writing, Tannen shows why women and men can walk away from the same conversation with completely different impressions of what was said. Studded with lively and entertaining examples of actual conversations, this book gives you the tools to understand what went wrong—and find a common language to strengthen relationships at work and at home. A classic in the field of interpersonal relations, this book will change forever the way you approach conversations.

Emotional Intelligence: Why It Can Matter More Than IQ, Daniel Goleman

Goleman's brilliant report from the frontiers of psychology and neuroscience offers startling new insight into our "two minds"—the rational and the emotional—and how they together shape our destiny. Drawing on groundbreaking brain and behavioral research, Goleman shows the factors at work when people of high IQ flounder and those of modest IQ do surprisingly well. These factors, which include self-awareness, self-discipline, and empathy, add up to a different way of being smart—and they aren't fixed at birth. Although shaped by childhood experiences, emotional intelligence can be nurtured and strengthened throughout adulthood—with immediate benefits to our health, relationships, and work.

How to Win Friends and Influence People, Dale Carnegie

Carnegie's first book is a timeless bestseller packed with rock-solid advice that has carried thousands of now-famous people up the ladder of success in their business and personal lives. As relevant as ever, Carnegie's principles endure and will help you achieve your maximum potential in the complex and competitive modern age. Learn the 6 ways to make people like you, the 12 ways to win people to your way of thinking, and the 9 ways to change people without arousing resentment.

Chapter 10: Leadership and Management

On Becoming a Leader, Warren Bennis

Dubbed the "dean of leadership gurus" by *Forbes* magazine, Bennis remains the final word in modern leadership. This seminal work is a must-read for anyone who aspires to leadership excellence. Warren Bennis (1925–2014) was a pioneer in leadership studies, a scholar who advised presidents and business executives on how to become successful leaders. Bennis's core belief is that leaders are not born—they are made. Providing essential and timeless insights for generations of readers, *On Becoming a Leader* delves into the qualities that define leadership, the people who exemplify it, and the strategies anyone can apply to achieve it.

As We Speak: How to Make Your Point and Have It Stick, Peter Meyers and Shann Nix

This is a practical and empowering guide to becoming a more effective, persuasive communicator. Whether you are speaking to a large audience, within a group, or in a one-on-one conversation, how you communicate ideas, as much as the ideas themselves, can determine success or failure. The book covers three core principles: Content: Construct a clear and lucid architecture of ideas that will lead your listener through a memorable emotional experience. Delivery: Use your voice and body to engage your audience and naturally support your message. State: Bring yourself into peak performance condition. How you feel when performing is the most frequently overlooked component of communication.

Peak: How Great Companies Get Their Mojo from Maslow, Chip Conley

Part memoir, part theory, and part application, *Peak* tells of Joie de Vivre's remarkable transformation while providing real-world examples from other companies and showing how readers can bring about similar changes in their work and personal lives. Applying psychologist Abraham Maslow's iconic hierarchy of needs, Conley explains how to understand the motivations of employees, customers, bosses, and investors and use that understanding to foster better relationships and build an enduring and thriving corporate culture.

The One Minute Manager, Kenneth Blanchard and Spencer Johnson

The One Minute Manager ranks as one of the most successful management books ever published. The strategies of one-minute management can save time and increase productivity, whether in business, at home, or even managing children. It covers three management techniques: One Minute Goal Setting, One Minute Praising, and One Minute Reprimands. Deceptively simple and measurably effective, applying these techniques can boost profits, productivity, and purpose.

Beyond Entrepreneurship: Turning Your Business into an Enduring Great Company, James Collins and William Lazier

This inspiring work provides entrepreneurs and other leaders with building blocks to help their companies and organizations sustain high performance, play a leadership role in their industries, and remain great for generations. The book includes real-world examples from Nike, L.L.Bean, Walmart, Federal Express (FedEx), and other success stories.

Made to Stick: Why Some Ideas Survive and Others Die, Chip Heath and Dan Heath

This book explains how some ideas influence their audience, making a mark on their memory for a long time and even spurring them to act, while others are forgotten, having hardly been heard. The authors of Made to Stick study the ideas that stick and explain their methods of adhesion. When marketing anything, keep these six concepts in mind if you want your message to stick: Simple, Unexpected, Concrete, Credible, and Emotional Stories; that spells SUCCESs.

Chapter 11: Charity, Philanthropy, and Service

Wealthy and Wise: How You and America Can Get the Most out of Your Giving, Claude Rosenberg Jr.

Citing an economy-boosting $80 billion per year potential in charitable funds, financial management expert Claude Rosenberg Jr. offers practical and tax-saving guidelines for philanthropists at every income level.

Preparing Heirs: Five Steps to a Successful Transition of Family Wealth and Values, Roy Williams and Vic Preisser

Preparing Heirs offers clear, concise, well-organized, and easy-to-follow instructions that will enable you to evaluate your plan for transitioning family wealth. It can help prepare your heirs to be good stewards and thoughtful administrators of that wealth. *Preparing Heirs* discloses the findings from research into the legacies of 3,250 wealthy families. It reveals how they achieved and maintained family harmony and ensured the smooth transition of their wealth to well-adjusted heirs. The authors also warn of the many factors that cause most wealthy families to fail in their transition. The book can be used in conjunction with the services of qualified professionals such as attorneys and accountants.

Governance as Leadership: Reframing the Work of Nonprofit Boards, Richard Chait, William Ryan, and Barbara Taylor

Written by noted consultants and researchers attuned to the needs of practitioners, *Governance as Leadership* redefines nonprofit governance. It provides a powerful framework for a new covenant between trustees and executives: more macrogovernance in exchange for less micromanagement. Informed by theories that have transformed the practice of organizational leadership, this book sheds new light on the board's traditional fiduciary and strategic work. It introduces a critical third dimension of effective trusteeship: generative governance. It serves as both a resource of fresh approaches to familiar territory and a lucid guide to significant new territory. It provides a road map that leads nonprofit trustees and executives to governance as leadership.

Power and Love: A Theory and Practice of Social Change, Adam Kahane

For 20 years, Kahane worked around the world on many tough and vital challenges: food security, health care, economic development, judicial reform, peacemaking, and climate change. In this extraordinary book, he draws on this experience to delve deeply into the dual natures of both power and love, exploring their subtle and intricate interplay. With disarming honesty, Kahane relates how, through trial and error, he learned to balance them and offers practical guidance for how others can learn that balance as well.

Chapter 12: Conservation and the Environment

Braiding Sweetgrass: Indigenous Wisdom, Scientific Knowledge, and the Teachings of Plants, Robin Wall Kimmerer

This is an inspired weaving of indigenous knowledge, plant science, and personal narrative from a botanist, distinguished science professor, and Native American. Kimmerer makes a central argument: awakening the wider ecological consciousness requires acknowledging and celebrating our reciprocal relationship with the world. Once we begin to listen for the languages of other beings, we can start to understand the innumerable life-giving gifts the world provides us and learn to offer our thanks, our care, and our own gifts in return. And she captures beauty all along the way—the images of giant cedars and wild strawberries, a forest in the rain, and a meadow of fragrant sweetgrass.

The Wolverine Way, Douglas Chadwick

The Wolverine Way reveals the natural history of this species and the forces that threaten its future, engagingly told by Douglas Chadwick, who volunteered with the Glacier Wolverine Project. This five-year study in Glacier National Park—which involved dealing with blizzards, grizzlies, sheer mountain walls, and other daily challenges to survival—uncovered missing information about the wolverine's habitat, social structure, and reproduction habits. Wolverines, according to Chadwick, are the land equivalent of polar bears regarding the impacts of global warming. The plight of wolverines adds to the call for wildlife corridors that connect existing habitats.

American Wolf: A True Story of Survival and Obsession in the West, Nate Blakeslee

With novelistic detail, Blakeslee tells the gripping story of wolves. Once abundant in North America, these majestic creatures were hunted to near extinction in the lower 48 states by the 1920s. But in recent decades, conservationists have brought wolves back to the Rockies, igniting a battle over the very soul of the West. Following one pack, *American Wolf* describes their challenges on all fronts: by hunters, who compete with wolves for the elk they both prize; by cattle ranchers who are losing livestock and have the ear of politicians; and by other Yellowstone wolves who are vying for control of the park's stunningly beautiful Lamar Valley. Blakeslee tells a larger story about the ongoing cultural clash in the West—between those fighting for a vanishing way of life and those committed to restoring one of the country's most iconic landscapes.

Coyote America: A Natural and Supernatural History, Dan Flores

Flores does more than just shed light on the legend; he explores five million years of biological history that led up to the evolution of the modern coyote and details the unique versatility of an animal that has continued to thrive despite human campaigns of annihilation. Legends don't come close to capturing the incredible story of the coyote. In the face of centuries of campaigns of annihilation employing gases, helicopters, and engineered epidemics, coyotes didn't just survive; they thrived, expanding across the continent from Alaska to New York. In the war between humans and coyotes, coyotes have won, hands down. It is one of the great epics of our time.

Biomimicry: Innovation Inspired by Nature, Janine Benyus

Biomimics study nature's most successful ideas over the past 3.5 million years and adapt them for human use. The results are revolutionizing how materials are invented and how we compute, heal ourselves, repair the environment, and feed the world. Benyus takes readers into the lab and in the field with maverick thinkers as they discover miracle drugs by watching what chimps eat when they're sick, learn how to create by watching spiders weave fibers, harness energy by examining how a leaf converts sunlight into fuel in trillionths of a second, and many more examples. Composed of stories of vision and invention, personalities and pipe dreams, *Biomimicry* is must reading for anyone interested in the shape of our future.

The Sustainability Revolution: Portrait of a Paradigm Shift, Andres Edwards

The Sustainability Revolution paints a picture of sustainability from the point of view of five major sectors of society: community (government and international institutions); commerce (business); resource extraction (forestry, farming, fisheries, etc.); ecological design (architecture, technology); and biosphere (conservation, biodiversity, etc.). Edwards explains a new set of values that define this paradigm shift. He describes innovative sustainable projects and policies in Colombia, Brazil, India, and the Netherlands and examines future trends. Complete with a valuable resource list, this book will appeal to business and government policymakers, academics, and all interested in sustainability.

Cradle to Cradle: Remaking the Way We Make Things, William McDonough and Michael Braungart

Elaborating on their principles from experience (re)designing everything from carpeting to corporate campuses, McDonough and Braungart make an exciting and viable case challenging the notion that human industry must inevitably damage the natural world. The customary advice to "do more with less in order to minimize damage" perpetuates a one-way, "cradle-to-grave" manufacturing model that casts off as much as 90 percent of the materials it uses as waste, much of which is toxic. Instead, taking nature itself as our model, the authors argue, products might be designed so that, after their useful life, they provide nourishment for something new—either as "biological nutrients" that safely reenter the environment or as "technical nutrients" that circulate within closed-loop industrial cycles—without being "downcycled" into low-grade uses (as most "recyclables" now are).

The New Economy of Nature: The Quest to Make Conservation Profitable, Gretchen Daily and Katherine Ellison

The New Economy of Nature brings together Gretchen Daily, one of the world's leading ecologists, with Katherine Ellison, a Pulitzer Prize–winning journalist, to offer an engaging and informative look at a new "new economy"—a system recognizing the economic value of natural systems and the potential profits in protecting them. Through engaging stories from around the world, the authors introduce readers to a diverse group of people pioneering new approaches to conservation. The authors describe the dynamic interplay of science, economics, business, and politics in establishing these new approaches and examine what will be needed to create successful models and lasting institutions for conservation.

Let There Be Water: Israel's Solution for a Water-Starved World, Seth Siegel

Based on meticulous research and hundreds of interviews, *Let There Be Water* reveals the methods and techniques of the often offbeat inventors who enabled Israel to lead the world in cutting-edge water technology. Siegel gives an inspiring account of the vision and sacrifice of a nation and people that have long made water security a top priority. Despite scant natural water resources, a rapidly growing population and economy, and often hostile neighbors, Israel has consistently jumped ahead of the water innovation curve to ensure a dynamic, vital future for itself. As every day brings urgent reports of growing water shortages around the world, there is no time to lose in the search for solutions.

The Ecology of Commerce: A Declaration of Sustainability, Paul Hawken

Hawken's impassioned argument is that business both causes the most egregious abuses of the environment and, crucially, holds the most potential for solving our sustainability problems. *The Ecology of Commerce* presents a compelling vision of the restorative (rather than destructive) economy we must create, centered on eight imperatives: reduce energy carbon emissions 80 percent by 2030 and total natural resource usage 80 percent by 2050; provide secure, stable, and meaningful employment to people everywhere; be self-organizing rather than regulated or morally mandated; honor market principles; restore habitats, ecosystems, and societies to their optimum; rely on current income; be fun and engaging; and strive for an aesthetic outcome.

Awakening Earth: Exploring the Evolution of Human Culture and Consciousness, Duane Elgin

Bringing together views from science and spirituality, East and West, the practical and the visionary, Elgin presents a balanced picture of human evolution—and explores three additional stages of development that must still be realized if we are to become a planetary civilization that can endure into the distant future.

The Future of Life, Edward Wilson

Wilson, one of the world's most important scientists, assesses the precarious state of our environment, examining the mass extinctions occurring in our time and the natural treasures we are about to lose forever. Yet, rather than trumpeting doomsday prophecies, he spells out a specific plan to save our world while there is still time. His vision is a hopeful one, as economically sound as it is environmentally necessary. Eloquent, practical, and wise, this book should be read and studied by anyone concerned about the fate of the natural world.

Diet for a New America: How Your Food Choices Affect Your Health, Happiness, and the Future of Life on Earth, John Robbins

Diet for a New America is the most comprehensive argument for a vegetarian lifestyle ever published. Eloquently, evocatively, and entertainingly, Robbins examines the food we currently buy and eat in the United States and the moral, economic, and emotional price we pay for it. He looks hard at our dependence on animals for food and the inhumane conditions these animals are raised in. He challenges the belief that consuming meat is a requirement for health by pointing out the vastly increased rate of disease caused by pesticides, hormones, additives, and other chemicals now a routine part of our food production. Robbins concludes that consuming the resources necessary to produce meat is a significant factor in our ecological crisis.

Chapter 13: Evolving—Aging with Soul

Switch: How to Change Things When Change Is Hard, Chip Heath and Dan Heath

Why is it so hard to make lasting changes in our companies, communities, and lives? *Switch* shows that successful changes follow a pattern you can use to make the changes that matter to you, whether your interest is in changing the world or changing your waistline.

Chapter 14: Gaining Wisdom

Becoming Wise: An Inquiry into the Mystery and Art of Living, Krista Tippett

In *Becoming Wise*, Krista Tippett has created a master class on living in a fractured world. Fracture, she says, is not the whole story of our time. The enduring question of what it means to be human has become inextricable from the challenge of who we are to one another. She insists on the possibility of personal depth, nurtured by science and "spiritual technologies," with civility and love as muscular public practice. This book is for people who want to take up the great questions of our time with imagination and courage to nurture new realities in the spaces we inhabit, doing so expectantly and with joy.

What I Wish I Knew When I Was 20: A Crash Course on Making Your Place in the World, Tina Seelig

As head of the Stanford Technology Ventures Program, Seelig shares with us what she offers her students—provocative stories, inspiring advice, and a hefty dose of humility and humor. The book is filled with fascinating examples, from the classroom to the boardroom, of individuals defying expectations, challenging assumptions, and achieving unprecedented success. Seelig throws out the old rules and provides a new model for reaching our potential. We discover how to have a healthy disregard for the impossible, how to recover from failure, and how most problems are remarkable opportunities in disguise.

Ethical Wills: Putting Your Values on Paper, Barry Baines, MD

A comprehensive, step-by-step resource, *Ethical Wills* gently guides us through the process of creating what can be one of the most valuable and cherished documents we leave behind. Clarifying and communicating the meaning of our lives for those who survive us, an ethical will helps us reflect on and share our life experiences. Those who want to be remembered authentically and for their gifts of heart, mind, and spirit will take satisfaction in knowing that what they value most is "on the record" and not to be lost or forgotten. *Ethical Wills* helps readers create, preserve, and share this important document with friends and family.

Old Friend from Far Away: The Practice of Writing Memoir, Natalie Goldberg

Goldberg is a foremost writing teacher and completely transforms the practice of writing a memoir. Through timed, associative, and meditative exercises, *Old Friend from Far Away* guides you to the attentive state of thought in which you discover and open forgotten doors of memory. At once a beautifully written celebration of the memoir form, an innovative course full of practical teachings, and a deeply affecting meditation on consciousness, love, life, and death, *Old Friend from Far Away* welcomes aspiring writers of all levels. It encourages them to find their unique voice to tell their stories.

ACKNOWLEDGMENTS

Our lives are filled with firsts—the first day of school, the first time we read a book on our own, the first romantic kiss. While I love reading and do so every day, until I started writing this book—my first—frankly, I didn't know much about writing, editing, and publishing a book. Yes, I have written a tremendous number of papers of various lengths, including a senior thesis in college, several white papers, and hundreds of business memoranda for clients. But writing a book for the public is an entirely different thing.

I could not have written my first book without the encouragement of many fabulous people all along the way. From simple positive comments to a sense of interest and excitement and regular check-ins, this meant a huge amount to me, and candidly, without it, I might have stopped the process before the end.

I received considerable help, assistance, and feedback in writing this book. Somehow, I wisely knew I needed to send a first serious draft (a manuscript, if you will) to three people who knew me well and were willing to read and give me critically valuable feedback. Thank you, Faruq Ahmad, whom I met at business school many decades ago. He was our best man at our wedding and became "Uncle" Faruq to my two children. Thank you, Andres Edwards, whom I met decades ago while expanding my relationships with environmentalists. Andres is quite familiar with writing and publishing books and is one of the world's leaders in writing about sustainability. His knowledge and experience were of great value. Thank you, Joshua Kagen, who is a kindred soul, and we have established a depth of relationship that allows for vulnerability and extraordinary candor. Their voices of encouragement have been of enormous value. I am grateful beyond measure for the excellent and caring assistance my first three readers provided.

Once I had a more developed draft, I began exploring the world of editing and publishing. On a hike up on Mt. Tamalpais, I met Heather Louise Barrett, who had been a literary editor for over 10 years. Among other important topics, I thank her for educating and gently prodding me about how I might market my book.

Andres Edwards introduced me to John Geoghegan. John has written and published several excellent books. His wise and thorough editorial comments and knowledge of the publishing world helped me make this book a reality.

On a trip to Palm Springs, my wife and I met Susan Keefe and her husband, Eric. Susan had recently retired from Oracle, and when I described my book, she offered to introduce me to a former colleague, Eric Maikranz, who had self-published a book that was made into a movie. When I connected with Eric, he gave me excellent recommendations about self-publishing my book, including, among many other things, asking beta readers to provide feedback. Sincere thanks to both Susan and Eric!

Bob Horn, a colleague for decades, is a visual language guru and author of several books. His gentle encouragement and helpful counsel were very appreciated. Old friends Doug Berenson, Steve Greene, Dean Meyer, and Gary Mills were voices of encouragement in the long process of writing and getting this book published. Thank you, my dear friends.

And an enormous thank-you to my wife, Carol. She is a central part of my choices in life, which have led to my thriving. I thank you wholeheartedly for being my partner through life's many adventures.

I very much appreciate the encouragement and guidance Matt Mead gave me and the production work lead by Jordyn Feyen.

And besides the people above, to whom I am deeply grateful, I want to acknowledge one more thing: COVID-19. I began writing this book near the beginning of the great pandemic in May 2020. During what I call the Great Pause, I had more time to quietly start the immense task of pulling together the elements that make up this book. Frankly, without having this period foisted upon me, I don't know when I would have been able to write this book. Please make no mistake, this is not a thank-you but merely an acknowledgment of how events out of our control and often unexpected and unwanted can lead to positive places.

ABOUT THE AUTHOR

Rand Selig has an MBA from Stanford and earned undergraduate degrees in mathematics and psychology. He has managed hundreds of complex projects in his career and has run his own financial services firm for over 35 years. He has lived and worked in Europe, Asia, Mexico, and the Caribbean.

He was a Little League coach and Scoutmaster and has served on numerous boards for decades. He is a roll-up-your-sleeves conservationist committed to helping others and Mother Earth by making annual philanthropic contributions.

This book is based on extensive research and a wide range of experiences he has had going through life. Having a high set point for happiness and being relentlessly positive has been invaluable to him in overcoming his challenges and setbacks. He is committed to personal growth and is willing to learn from his mistakes. Rand believes he can design his own life and believes others can too.

Rand takes time every week to rest and recharge. He loves reading, watching movies, hiking, and playing tennis. He lives with his wife of 42 years in Mill Valley, California. They have two children and two granddaughters. He loves and is enormously grateful for the life he has been lent.

Rand welcomes comments and suggestions for this book. Please visit his website at www.randselig.com